Jim Thorpe

World's Greatest Athlete

by Gregory B. Richards

 CHILDRENS PRESS ™

CHICAGO

DEDICATION

For my Parents

ACKNOWLEDGMENTS

Of particular interest to the author in preparing this book were two detailed biographies which are "must" reading for those interested in knowing more of Jim Thorpe's story. They are *The Best of the Athletic Boys*, by Jack Newcombe, and *Jim Thorpe—World's Greatest Athlete*, by Robert W. Wheeler. Also of help was Jack Cusack's text, *Pioneer in Pro Football*, and back issues of the *New York Times*. The reference desk of the Learning Resources Center at the College of DuPage provided extended access to newspaper microfilms.

Special thanks are given to Childrens Press editors Fran Dyra and Mary Reidy for their patience; my father, Norman Richards, for his encouragement; and my wife, Tari, for somehow putting up with it all— and still smiling.

PICTURE ACKNOWLEDGMENTS

United Press International—2, 59; Brown Brothers—52, 54, 55, 58; Culver Pictures, Inc.—53; Associated Press—56; The Grace Thorpe Collection—57, 58 (inset) Cover illustration by Len W. Meents

Library of Congress Cataloging in Publication Data

Richards, Gregory B.
  Jim Thorpe, world's greatest athlete.

  Bibliography: p.
  Includes index.
  Summary: A biography of Jim Thorpe, one of the greatest all-around athletes in history.
  1. Thorpe, Jim, 1887-1953—Juvenile literature.
2. Athletes—United States—Biography—Juvenile literature.
[1. Thorpe, Jim, 1887-1953. 2. Athletes. 3. Indians of North America—Biography] I. Title.
GV697.T5R53 1984   796'.092'4 [B] [92]   84-14240
ISBN 0-516-03207-0

Table of Contents

FOREWORD

As one of Jim Thorpe's daughters from his first marriage to Iva Margaret Miller, I recall my father's sports history by remembering our personal family events. For example, Mother graduated from Carlisle Indian School in Pennsylvania in March of 1912, a few months before Dad won the decathlon and pentathlon in the summer Olympics held in Stockholm, Sweden.

After their marriage at Carlisle in October, 1913, they spent their honeymoon sailing around the world on a goodwill tour with the New York Giants. Dad was still playing with the Giants when Jim, Jr., was born in New York City in 1915.

Dad sold his Sac and Fox Indian allotted lands south of Prague, Oklahoma, and with the money bought the only home he ever owned, about forty miles north in Yale, where my sister Gail was born in 1917. Charlotte was born two years later when he was playing with the Boston Braves baseball team in Massachusetts.

In 1921, I was born in Yale at the Jim Thorpe Home, now a museum operated by the State of Oklahoma Historical Society. (Plans are underway for a memorial across the street.) Professional football was just getting started in Ohio then and Dad was the first elected president of the American Professional Football Association, now the National Football League.

He was in his middle thirties when I was born. I can recall him standing at center field at the Haskell Institute football stadium in Lawrence, Kansas, where I was a five-year-old student. He kicked a football through one goalpost, then turned around and easily kicked another ball to the goalpost at the other end.

Unfortunately the glory, fame, and recognition of his athletic accomplishments did not bring him happiness. His personal life was sad, but he learned to overcome tragedy and still perform.

At age nine he lost his twin brother, Charlie, who died of small-pox and pneumonia. Only five of his brothers and sisters grew to adulthood. In 1901 his mother died of complications during child-birth and he was an orphan at sixteen when his father died of blood poisoning. Tragedy continued in his adult life—Jim, Jr., only two-and-a-half, died in his arms; my mother divorced him; and Freeda Kirkpatrick, his second wife, divorced him after the birth of four sons, Carl Philip, William, Richard, and John.

Through all this, though, he kept his smile and did not lose his sense of humor, which was probably his greatest emotional asset.

Most famous people are rich. Dad was one of the few who were not. All his glory and fame did not bring him riches. Indeed, in his later years, although he lived modestly, he still had problems paying his bills.

In spite of all his personal problems, he was a successful man in his field. He was not a businessman and never learned how to exploit his fame. However, businessmen were in awe of him because they didn't know how to be athletes either. He achieved his success in the world of sports. Because of his overwhelming success in sports he achieved what few do—he achieved immortality. The name Jim Thorpe will live in the hearts of sports-minded people forever.

Grace F. Thorpe

Chapter 1

WORLD'S GREATEST ATHLETE

The crowd fell quiet. All thirty thousand sports enthusiasts leaned forward in their seats, their eyes on the track that ran around the double-tiered stadium. Seven athletes crouched in tension on the cinder path, their eyes focused on the track ahead of them, their ears listening for the sound of the starting gun.

It was growing late that Sunday afternoon of July 7, 1912, and the competitors in the Olympic 1,500-meter race at Stockholm, Sweden, were beginning to ache with fatigue. They were entered in the pentathlon, a demanding five-event track and field contest, and the mile-long footrace was the final test.

Dominating the competition so far was Jim Thorpe, renowned athlete from Carlisle Indian School in Pennsylvania, a football and track star who had captured the world's attention as an incredibly talented, all-around athlete. The year before, Thorpe had distinguished himself as the greatest halfback and kicker in collegiate football. He had led the squad from the tiny Indian school in victories against giants—the University of Pennsylvania and even the "unstoppable" Harvard.

Now the attention of millions was turned to this fifth modern Olympiad in Stockholm—to see if twenty-five-year-old Thorpe and his American teammates could prove themselves against Scandinavian athletes, thought to be some of the world's strongest runners. The 1,500-meter run, in particular, was considered to be a sure thing for Hugo Wieslander, an impressive Swedish trackman. The Swedes in the grandstand were hoping that in this final event the tide could be turned against Thorpe's threat.

The piercing starting shot rang out and the seven runners sprang forward. Thorpe was positioned in the next-to-outside running lane, a disadvantage, and loped off to a slow start. American runner Avery Brundage and Ferdinand Bie of Norway dashed off to struggle for an early lead in the three-lap race. Both runners kept that lead throughout the first lap, with the rest of the pack trailing behind.

Well behind them all was Thorpe. The spectators stirred in bewilderment. Why, they asked, was this so-called athletic superman lagging? But Thorpe knew. He was deliberately pacing himself, saving strength and waiting to make his move for the lead.

In the middle of the second lap, Bie had captured the lead, and Thorpe sensed that it was time to take him on. By the start of the third and final lap, Thorpe had sprinted up to Bie's position. Now, the fiery kick in Bie's step that made him famous was disappearing, just as Thorpe had anticipated.

The Norwegian was growing tired! Without even glancing over his shoulder, the American burst forward, leaving Bie behind him.

It was Thorpe who, to the deafening cheers of the crowd, flung himself first into the finish-line tape several yards ahead of the closest contenders. Thorpe stole the day with feats of speed and endurance throughout the five events, establishing a record that has never been topped.

His charge for victory went still further. Thorpe conquered an even more challenging event, the decathlon, in the next few days. No athlete had ever triumphed before in so many different events. His talents silenced European critics, who had portrayed American athletes as specialists, lacking the versatility of true champions. And, said one United States official, "It also answers the allegation that most of our runners are of foreign parentage, for Thorpe is a real American if ever there was one."

At the presentation of the gold medals, Thorpe stepped up twice before King Gustav V of Sweden. A reporter for the *New York Times* described the scene: "When James Thorpe, the Carlisle Indian and finest all-around athlete in the world, appeared to claim the prizes for winning the pentathlon, there was a great burst of cheers, led by the king. The immense crowd cheered itself hoarse."

Gustav then placed the laurel wreath atop Thorpe's head, hung the gold medal around his neck, and presented him with a four-foot bronze bust, made in the king's likeness. Later, as Jim Thorpe received prizes for his decathlon win, the king took the young man's hand and proclaimed, "Sir, you are the greatest athlete in the world."

The crowd's elation would have been greatly dimmed had they known what was to come for Jim Thorpe. Just six months later, Thorpe was to be charged with taking money for playing baseball during a college break. Branded a professional, he was to be stripped of his amateur status and his name erased from the record books. Worst of all, his gold medals and trophies were to be taken back, to leave Thorpe crushed by disappointment.

Jim Thorpe's life story is filled with twists. He countered his disgrace in later years with phenomenal success as a gridiron ball player, both in collegiate and early professional football. He fought to avoid slipping into the obscurity to which so many athletes are destined. Most important, his family and supporters never gave up their battle to restore the Olympic records and medals he had won.

In spite of the events that shaped his bittersweet career, though, Thorpe was never deprived of his title, "World's Greatest Athlete." Perhaps he never will be.

Chapter 2

SURVIVAL IN INDIAN TERRITORY

One of the characteristics that has made Jim Thorpe a fascinating figure is his Indian heritage. His background, some have said, endowed Thorpe with a fierce sense of pride and an appreciation for physical activity. He especially loved competition calling for bodily speed, agility, and strength, traits for which his ancestral Sac and Fox tribe is known.

Of course, those qualities and the physical prowess that Thorpe possessed are not unique to any one race. Those same factors have enabled athletes of other races to perform remarkable feats and even to achieve fame. But Thorpe's experience as a part Indian, made to conform to the ways of the white world, and his upbringing in the harsh surroundings of the Oklahoma Territory played a big role in forming the personal traits needed for success.

Perhaps Jim's ability to survive hardship was a gift of his hardy grandfather, Hiram G. Thorpe, an Irish blacksmith who traveled from Connecticut to the midwestern frontier in the early 1800s to forge a living as a trader and fur trapper. Thorpe chose to settle with the Sac and Fox Indians. In the early 1840s, the tribe had been moved by the

United States government from its homeland in the upper Mississippi Valley in Iowa and northern Illinois to territory in Kansas.

The Sac and Fox Indians were Woodland Indians native to the Great Lakes and the rich, green pastures and river valleys of the Midwest. Those tribes were the target of a large-scale removal effort by the government. Such territory was tempting to citizens from the East who wanted their own land, and the government aimed to dole it out to them. Between 1825 and 1840, more than 100,000 Indians were prodded, negotiated, and sometimes tricked or forcibly pushed toward the flat prairies west of the Mississippi River. The idea was to establish the Great Plains as the homeland of all Indians, out of the way of white homesteaders moving westward.

The Sac and Fox Indians, like many other tribes, resented the idea of leaving their homelands. In the bloody Black Hawk War of 1832, they fought fiercely to keep their land. The conflict, named after the famed Sac and Fox warrior Black Hawk, ended in a massacre of hundreds of tribal warriors, women, and children—and with the breaking of the people's aggressive spirit.

The prize for the government was a treaty that forced the Sac and Fox to sell a huge strip of land along the Mississippi River. Today the eastern half of Iowa, that land included ten million of perhaps the world's most fertile acres. In return, the tribe received $600,000, paid over thirty years; a large sum of cash; quarterly annuity payments of cash to each tribal member; some supplies, including cloth, tobacco, and salt; and blacksmith and gunsmith shops for the reservation lands in Kansas. It was Hiram Thorpe, Jim's grandfather, who landed the government job of blacksmith.

Hiram Thorpe soon married into the Sac and Fox tribe, as did many other traders and workers who settled in or near the reservation. The Sac and Fox elders, including Chief Black Hawk, had long since given up trying to discourage the mixing of white blood into the tribe, and for many white men, an Indian wife was a source of stability and practical comforts. An Indian woman named No-ten-o-quah, or "Wind Woman," a member of the Thunder Clan to which Black Hawk also belonged, married Thorpe shortly after his arrival in Kansas in 1842.

In the early years of their marriage, Thorpe and No-ten-o-quah witnessed many changes in the ways members of the Indian community supported themselves. There were changes, too, in the way Indians lived with the white men.

Before being separated from their homelands, the Sac and Fox had thrived on a combination of skillful farming and long winter hunts for wild game. The women had been responsible for planting and harvesting plentiful fields of corn. They had also cared for beans, squashes, and other crops in community gardens and had looked after the young.

Men in the tribe had journeyed westward in the late winter and again in the summer in search of buffalo and other wild prey. Buffalo were plentiful then, and the green, well-watered region of the Mississippi Valley was ideal for cultivating vegetables.

But life on the Indian reservation in Kansas didn't lend itself to the same sort of livelihood. The climate itself was much more severe; a drought in 1850, for example, wiped out hundreds of acres of corn, the year's entire crop. And as the homesteading rush of white people into the area got in the way of the Indians' periodic hunts, the vital supplies of buffalo meat and hides became increasingly scarce. Worse yet, different tribes were having to compete for their winter kill, and buffalo herds were beginning to thin. It was the first sign of an eventual extinction of the country's buffalo population, a condition that would mean disaster for many Indian tribes.

Less able to support themselves, the Sac and Fox became more reliant on the government agency's annuity payments. The size of those payments depended on the number of persons in each household, and in that regard, Hiram Thorpe was well-off. Within a few years, No-ten-o-quah bore six children, including a son, Hiram P., in 1850.

The younger Hiram was one of the first half-blooded Indians to be educated in the white man's style. The boy was one of a handful of students attending the agency's first school.

There were hundreds of eligible school-age children in the tribe, but most were kept at home by Sac and Fox parents, who were suspicious of such education. They feared that once behind classroom doors, their children would be forced to take up another religion.

Only a few years after Hiram and his classmates had settled into their routine at the agency school, the Sac and Fox tribe was dealt a final blow by the government. The press of white settlers into Missouri and Kansas whetted the government's appetite for the prairie lands it had promised to the Indians and their heirs only a few years before. In 1869, the Indians were "asked" to sell their Kansas reserve, which had already been whittled down in size, in exchange for one dollar per acre plus a parcel of land in Indian Territory. This land would later be called Oklahoma Territory.

With the bitter memory of past treaties and land swindles in mind, many Indians refused to move; some joined remnants of other Sac and Fox groups farther east. Only a fraction of the tribe that had been moved to Kansas—four hundred out of the original two thousand—made the trip by federally escorted wagons to Oklahoma that winter. That small remnant of the Sac and Fox population, which only a half century before had numbered in the thousands and which had reigned over most of the upper Midwest, found its new home to be a semiarid, seventeen-by-forty-mile strip of dusty Oklahoma land.

For the Thorpe family, the fight for survival again meant dependence on annuities from the government. At least with fewer tribal people to share the money, there was more to go around. That wasn't always the case with food. Crops the Indians knew how to plant could not survive the hot, dry weather and poor soil; and wild game was hard to come by in a landscape now dominated by cattle from Europe.

The remaining Sac and Fox would again have to adjust to a new environment in order to survive. That wasn't an easy proposition in a winter plagued by bitter cold, hunger, and illness. Also the government's Bureau of Indian Affairs was attempting to bolster its long-term efforts to "civilize" its "savage" wards. The agency tried, without much success, to prohibit gambling, a long-favored Sac and Fox pastime, and the trading or drinking of liquor. Drinking was foreign to the Indian heritage, but visitors from other cultures had used it to tempt Indians or make them too drunk to scrutinize treaties over the years. What the visitors did not teach the Indians was the danger of alcohol addiction. Sadly, many Indians became alcoholics.

The biggest change imposed upon the Indians came in 1887 when the government decided that a frontier could no longer be defined. Growing numbers of white settlers were making great demands for land—even Indian reservations— previously considered as wilderness. As a result, the Indians were told to stop thinking of land as a gift of nature, communal property that belonged to everyone. Each was given a deed for a 160-acre section of land, plus $250 toward the purchase of leftover Indian territory. That area, too, was soon opened to settlers in the land run of September 1891. The whites scurried onto the scene, dotting the landscape with covered wagons and hammering claim stakes into the ground.

But young Hiram P. Thorpe was particularly well suited to survive the changes around him. He had grown into a strapping, muscular man, standing more than six feet tall and weighing well over two hundred pounds. Like his Indian forefathers, Hiram loved physical challenges. He became known among the Sac and Fox as the best wrestler, swimmer, and rider for miles around. He was the undisputed champion of almost any sports contest.

Hiram was also highly prolific; he fathered some nineteen children in his time, by five women. The Sac and Fox Indians, like other tribes, believed in a polygamous way of marriage. Men commonly took more than one wife, and marriages were sometimes brief, with separation being a simple and accepted way of parting. Not long after arriving in Oklahoma, Hiram married his first wife, a Shawnee Indian named Mary James. Hiram and Mary settled on the Sac and Fox reservation in the Oklahoma Territory, where they had four children.

By the time the General Allotment Act, which called for individual ownership of land, was passed in 1887, Hiram had taken no fewer than three wives. His third was Charlotte Vieux, a great granddaughter of Jacques Vieux, a French fur trader who founded Milwaukee, Wisconsin, and granddaughter of Potawatomi Chief Louis Vieux. Hiram and Charlotte, as did a few other families, built a small cabin on the banks of the North Canadian River near Keokuk Falls, which provided better feeding areas for livestock and better soil for crops. It was in that small cabin, crafted of wood from native cottonwood and pecan trees, that their son George was born and five years later, on May 22, 1887, a pair of twins, Charles and James. Their birth date is recorded on the Sacred Heart Church register in Konawa, Oklahoma, on the Potawatomi Reservation.

At the time, it wasn't unusual for children to die within a few years of birth. In fact, Hiram and Charlotte had already lost twin daughters a few years before Jim's birth. But Jim and Charlie were robust babies. Each weighed more than nine pounds and was able to resist the illnesses that often descended upon the Sac and Fox people.

Two years after the twins' birth, the Thorpes moved into a larger home, built of sanded boards, on their new land allotment along the North Canadian River. Here, the family was able to enjoy a comfortable existence. Hiram raised a good number of horses. He grew enough feed for the livestock and vegetables for the family. Corn, pumpkins, and beans helped keep the family fed. And like most Sac and

Fox men, Hiram was an excellent rifle shot and brought home occasional deer and fowl for their meat and hides.

For Jim and Charlie, life on the seemingly endless allotment acres was a series of outdoor adventures. There were Indian games to play, games like "Follow the Leader" and "Fox and Geese"; there were swimming, fishing, and hunting. "Our lives were lived out in the open," Jim later recalled, "winter and summer. We were never in the house when we could be out of it. And we played hard."

That vigorous life-style was the foundation of Jim's athletic development. True, there were no organized sports and no one to coach Jim and his playmates, but the children were learning what agility, stamina, and endurance meant in competition.

Jim and Charlie also gained an appreciation for outdoor living. By the time he was eight or nine, Jim was already making overnight camp alone, usually taking along an old hunting dog as a companion. "I became well versed in forest lore," Jim said. "I particularly loved to hunt and fish. I learned how to wait beside a runway and stalk a deer. I learned how to trap for bear and rabbits, coon and possum." Hiram taught the boys how to make snares from cornstalks to catch quail and, when Jim felled his first deer, how to dress and bring the catch home. As was the Indian practice, the Thorpes never hunted what was not needed for food.

As much as Jim loved the outdoors, he hated the prospect

of being shipped off to the agency's mission boarding school near Stroud, almost twenty-five miles away from home. Charlie and he were required to attend at the early age of six. The twins entered the first primary class in 1893, along with about sixty other Indian and part-Indian children of varying ages and tribal backgrounds, with boys and girls setting up quarters in separate dormitories. Half the school day was spent in the study of reading and writing, simple geography, and United States history. The other half consisted of so-called industrial training, which for Jim included farming chores.

The part of school that made Jim, like so many other Indian schoolchildren, hate being there was the discipline. The government believed that the only way to break in Indians to white culture was through a strict regime. Pupils were made to wear suits of dark clothing and heavy, black felt hats. The ringing of bells signaled all activities, including meals. Monotonous labor and close, constant supervision, even at playtime, marked each day. And the use of Indian languages was strictly forbidden. Any child daring to break the rules met with swift, and sometimes harsh, discipline.

Jim disliked school enough to run away and return home during his third year there. Hiram, being one of the few members of the Sac and Fox community who could read and write English, believed in education. He wasn't pleased to see Jim at his door. If nothing else, the boarding school was a good way to lower the cost of supporting Hiram's growing family. After some firm discipline of his own, Hiram deposited Jim back at the school.

By now, the teachers there had documented the differences between the twins. Charlie had slightly darker skin and brown hair and weighed a bit less than Jim. His instructors considered him a good student, with a mild, friendly disposition. Jim, on the other hand, had lighter skin and black hair, a prominent chin, and a restless, almost rebellious, nature. One teacher even called him an "incorrigible youngster." In class, Jim's mind often turned to dreams of outdoor life.

One of the few things that kept Jim from running wild was his older brother George—also attending the school— whom Jim respected. Perhaps another was the frequently played game of baseball, prairie-style, which had been introduced by white settlers. It was at that game and other running and jumping games, invented during the students' precious free time, that Jim excelled.

Jim might have improved as a student, as well, if tragedy hadn't touched his life. An epidemic of measles and other diseases broke out in the school late in the winter of 1897, when the twins were nine years old. Charlie was stricken with pneumonia and smallpox and at the time little was known about curing the victims. Jim's twin died in early March, leaving a lonely and upset brother behind. Jim returned home for the summer, but when he went back to school in the fall, his teachers saw that he had become more withdrawn and sullen than ever.

Jim had lost more than a family member; he had lost a lifelong playmate and one of his few inspirations for sticking with the school routine. Not surprisingly, Jim ran away from school again the following spring. This time, Hiram was determined to send Jim so far away from home that he wouldn't be able to find his way back.

During the summer, Hiram obtained information through the Sac and Fox agency about the Haskell Institute, situated in Lawrence, Kansas, hundreds of miles away. Boarded there were some six hundred Indian students, living in a military-style complex that featured the usual Indian-education elements—manual labor, classroom instruction, and lots of discipline. Hiram arranged to have Jim sent there in the fall, convinced that the school could help straighten out the boy.

As Jim boarded the train for Kansas that September, he could not have been happy. The eleven-year-old was about to face some tough challenges, and Haskell represented the sort of rigid institution with which he would have to cope for the next fifteen years. But also awaiting Thorpe was a new white man's game that was to capture the youth's hopes and ultimately let him rise above the rest. That game was football.

Chapter 3

A PRODIGY DISCOVERED

During his long train ride to Haskell, the young Thorpe may have hoped for a more casual school atmosphere, but he certainly didn't find one when he got there. Like other Indian schools, Haskell was set up like a military academy. The strict regimentation, decided the government, would help the Indians to learn an orderly and "civilized" life-style. It was an ambitious plan, considering that the Indians came from almost a hundred different tribes, some of which resisted whites' ideas about education.

The curriculum already was familiar to Jim. Four hours of each day, which began with a shrill bugle reveille at 5:45 in the morning, were spent in manual training. Students studied a given vocation for six months and then were rotated to another class and taught another job. The skills taught included baking, tailoring, blacksmithing, farming, wagon building, and more. The other four hours in the day were spent in the classroom learning the basics—history, mathematics, English, and science. The day ended with a bugler playing taps at 9:00 in the evening.

As at Jim's agency school in the Oklahoma Territory, students were disciplined if they used Indian language, were

24

caught roughhousing, came late to meals or assemblies, or were sloppy in appearance. They wore uniforms made at the school's tailor shop and were constantly reminded to keep their uniforms clean. Brass buttons and shoes alike were expected to shine at inspection time.

Jim found the environment uncomfortable at first. But by adjusting to it, he prepared himself well for more years of schooling later in life. The routine was not without some fun; baseball was a popular sport at Haskell, and Jim and his classmates spent many hours on the diamond. Jim loved the game and stood out from the others in his ability to learn its tricks. A keen sense of timing and coordination made him a good batter, while running speed and a strong throwing arm helped him succeed in the outfield.

But the sport that really caught Thorpe's eye was football. It had been introduced at Haskell shortly before his enrollment and had quickly gained popularity in nearby towns and schools. Jim and his friends liked to watch the older football players practice in the afternoons. Later the boys imitated the football players during improvised games at recess. The boys had only a homemade football to play with, but they were having too much fun clashing together in scrimmage to care.

Of special interest to Jim was Chauncey Archiquette, a huge quarterback on the Haskell varsity team. Simply by watching the older player, Jim learned some of the game's more sophisticated moves and practiced them later while playing with his own friends. Archiquette went on to play at Carlisle Indian School, the well-known college in Pennsylvania, a year or two later. It is not much of a surprise that Jim eventually followed Archiquette's example.

One of the most exciting times during Thorpe's years at school in Kansas was the visit of Carlisle's football team in January of 1900. Carlisle had just returned from a victory over the University of California. Haskell students put forth their best efforts for their visitors during parade exercises and at a special breakfast. Carlisle's players were celebrities to Haskell students, especially to those like Jim, who aspired to play on a college varsity team someday.

Thorpe not only found a niche for himself in sports but finally began to grasp some of the classroom subjects, too. He might have become an even better student if his stay at Haskell hadn't been interrupted in the summer of 1901 by some bad news. His father had been shot in a hunting accident. Without waiting for approval, Thorpe ran off to Lawrence's railroad yards, wearing his school work clothes. He hopped aboard a freight train, hoping to ride unnoticed to Oklahoma. After several hours, however, Jim was surprised to learn that the train was going north—the wrong way. He had to jump off. Jim spent the next two weeks walking and hitching rides all the way to Oklahoma, nearly three hundred miles away.

Finally arriving at home, Jim found his father almost recovered. Hiram had enough strength to show his displeasure at Jim's runaway behavior. The confused youth, probably wanting to prove that he could take care of himself, ran off again, this time to Texas. There was plenty of work on cattle ranges for someone who didn't mind helping out with horses and mending fences. Thorpe had learned to get along with horses at an early age in Oklahoma. His skill at handling them helped the fourteen-year-old earn enough money over several months to buy his own team of horses.

Hiram must have been very impressed the day Jim came riding back onto the Oklahoma farm, and the father and son made up. Jim was persuaded to return to the classroom, this time at Garden Grove, a local school. Life was made interesting by informal pickup baseball games in the nearby town of Bellmont, and time not spent in class or on the sandlot went to helping at home with younger brothers and sisters. This peaceful time was shattered, however, by another personal tragedy. On November 17, 1901 Jim's mother, Charlotte, died of complications from giving birth to her eleventh child, Henry, who died a few days later.

That loss was cause enough for Jim to be unhappy. Added to it was the fact that his relationship with Hiram, who remarried and began a new family not long after Charlotte's death, became strained over the following year. It is unclear who wanted more that Jim enroll in boarding school again;

whichever it was, Jim was soon signed up for Carlisle Indian School in distant Pennsylvania. The Sac and Fox agency having arranged for his train ticket to Carlisle, in February of 1904 Jim once again found himself on a lonely journey away from Oklahoma.

Now almost seventeen years old, Thorpe was used to military-style schools and was better prepared for Carlisle than were some of the younger Indian children enrolled there. The roll of students had reached almost a thousand by the time Jim arrived in early 1904. Most of the students had been sent by parents who were convinced of the value of a "white" education; others had been recruited for their athletic ability. Some people believe that Thorpe himself was accepted so that Carlisle's famous football coach, Glenn S. "Pop" Warner, could take a closer look at the Oklahoma sandlot slugger he had heard about.

The founder of the school, Lieutenant Richard Henry Pratt, knew that important friends in Washington and local groups would be impressed by a successful sports program. The average citizen of the day was caught up in the athletics craze; with few movies and no radio or television for pastimes, most people followed the sports scene with relish. The school's budget was tight, and in order for the government to continue supporting Carlisle, the approval of the public was vital. Pratt's answer was to build a top-notch athletic program.

Among the most popular sports at the larger universities was football. What better way to prove that Indians could compete as well as white men than to challenge them on the gridiron? Pratt decided that if Carlisle was to build a national reputation as a football-playing school, he would have to hire an outstanding coach. Pop Warner was the right man for the job. As a guard on Cornell University's football team, he had drawn public attention. After graduating, Warner had practiced law for a short while, but had yearned to get back on the football field. He had coached at Iowa State College and the University of Georgia before being drafted by Pratt in 1899 to work at Carlisle.

Warner was a driven, aggressive coach who demanded a lot from his players, sometimes with a harsh show of temper. The Indian athletes were at first put off by his gruff nature, and Warner was initially puzzled by their silent, low-key approach to football. But he soon learned that, treated with fairness, team spirit, and a measure of kindness, the Indians were totally loyal to their coach and the team and were fully devoted to the game. Warner later wrote in *Collier's* magazine:

> Carlisle had no traditions, but what the Indians did have was a real race pride and a fierce determination to show the [whites] what they could do when the odds were even. . . . Yet,

when it comes to sportsmanship, I never want to see a finer lot of thoroughbreds than those Indians. I saw them in games against famous universities where they were slugged viciously and purposely, yet, I can recall only one or two instances where an Indian repaid in kind.

Warner became famous as an innovator in football and probably did more to modernize the game than any other sportsman of his time. The double-wing formation, the spiral pass and spiral punt, and the three-point stance used by backs on the scrimmage line were all Warner innovations. He was a clever inventor as well, and during spare hours in school workshops turned out equipment such as blocking sleds, fiber padding for uniforms, and running shoes with cleats for playing on muddy fields. Most of all, he appreciated the willingness of the Indians to try new ideas and strategies. Warner later said that his teams at Carlisle had a "remarkable receptiveness to new ideas. . . the Carlisle bunch dearly loved to spring surprises and were happiest when I came forward with something different."

One of the most important new ideas was the body block. In previous football contests, the common method of blocking had used only the shoulder. Warner taught his men to leap over the ground, turning slightly so that they blocked their opponents with the hip. Various tricks were dreamed up, too, that allowed the Indians to keep the other team guessing as to the whereabouts of the ball during play.

The Indians' favorite, and the most famous, was "the hunchback play." In those days the entire team dropped back on kickoffs. The team formed a wedge or a wide V in front of the ballcarrier. The idea at kickoff was to send the receiver up the field with the football hidden in the back of his shirt. Running against the opposition with the rest of the team, the receiver would look as if he didn't have the ball. All that was needed to pull it off was a good long kick from the opposition and a running back with some extra elastic sewed in at the bottom of his jersey to hold the ball in place. The Indians endlessly practiced the trick in the 1903 season and finally put it to use against the famed Harvard team that fall. Pop Warner recalled in *Collier's* what happened when the right kickoff came Carlisle's way:

> The Indians gathered at once in what now would be called a huddle, but facing outward, and Johnson quickly slipped the ball under the back of Charlie Dillon's jersey. Charlie was picked as the "hunchback" because he stood six feet and could do a hundred yards in ten seconds. Besides, being a guard, he was less likely to be suspected of carrying the ball. The stands were in an uproar, for everybody had

seen the big lump on Dillon's back but the Harvard players were still scurrying wildly around when Charlie crossed the goal line. One of his mates jerked out the ball and laid it on the turf and, as I had warned the referee that the play might be attempted, he was watching carefully and ruled that the touchdown had been made within the rules.

The Carlisle Indians became a sensation in the football world during Warner's first year at the school. Pratt certainly got what he had bargained for. The team defeated Penn, a formidable match, and the whole country knew that the Indians had arrived. All of the football boys, as they were known on campus, were celebrities among the students. One can imagine the awe and admiration that Jim Thorpe, an athletically inclined youngster, must have had for the older players. More than anything, he must have wanted to be one of the football boys, too.

For the time being, Thorpe would have to be content with whatever small games he could fit in after his schoolwork. As at Haskell, the course load at Carlisle was divided evenly between manual training and classroom study. Thorpe was first enrolled in tailor-shop instruction. He looked forward eagerly to playing afternoon football in the "shop league," even though the matches with the bakers, printers, or carpenters were sometimes unorganized and clumsy. Thorpe was falling in love with the solid feeling of a smart dropkick and the rough-and-tumble play at the scrimmage line.

Thorpe was beginning to feel comfortable, too, with the Carlisle routine. Although the military regimentation there was extreme, it at least kept things running smoothly. Students wore army uniforms and practiced parade exercise with rifles and color guards. There were weekly inspections, of course, and boys and girls competed for the highest marks in dormitory neatness. What made Carlisle livable for many students was a feeling of school spirit and pride in both their academic and athletic accomplishments.

Once again, however, Thorpe's life was disrupted, this time with the news of his father's death as a result of blood poisoning. Jim felt lonelier than ever now that he had no parents to return to in Oklahoma. He was even too far away from home to attend the funeral. Assignment of a government guardian to manage his financial affairs was handled by mail. Thorpe's guardian continued to receive Jim's share of the government annuity payments due the Sac and Fox tribe and the income from rent on the land left to him by his parents.

Thorpe received enough money for essentials from his guardian; so, it was difficult for him to understand the need for his taking part in Lieutenant Pratt's "outing system." The idea of the program was to place Indian students on the farms of local white citizens for a few months during the summer or winter to learn more about the whites' domestic way of life. For the participating sponsors, the program also provided a source of relatively cheap labor; salaries ranged from five to ten dollars a month and were lower than those paid to white helpers. Half the money was sent to the college, where it was saved for the student.

Thorpe's first outing was to a farmer's house where he was made to clean house and help out in the kitchen—not a happy situation for someone who enjoyed the outdoors so much. However, some of the other assignments he received over his first three years put him in the field. If nothing else, Jim saw the outing as a way of getting out of the dormitory, where one hundred boys lived in close quarters. And the hard work helped build his physique. Upon arrival at Carlisle, the boy had stood five feet five inches tall, without much weight spread over his thin frame. Over a three-year period, he grew more than four inches and brought his weight up to 144 pounds. His tasks in the field had added some muscle, at least.

Thorpe was still not happy with the outing system. While on a field-chore assignment during the spring of 1907, he decided he had had enough and after a few weeks ran back to Carlisle. He was punished with a brief stay in the guardhouse, but the school superintendent decided not to send him back to the fields just yet. Thorpe was back in classes just in time for the school's annual Class Day, which coincided with Arbor Day. The event was filled with activity at the school, including nature walks and lectures, the planting of new trees on campus, and track-and-field competition. Thorpe was a standout on the sixth-grade team, adding to his reputation at Carlisle for athletic ability.

Fellow students certainly took notice when that sixth-grade team beat all of the higher-grade classes. Thorpe won the 120-yard hurdles, finishing in nineteen seconds, and the high jump, topping out at five feet nine inches. He finished in second place in the 220-yard dash. His victories practically assured him of a place on Carlisle's track squad. What clinched his placement on the team, though, was an impromptu tryout that took place one afternoon as Jim was on his way to a football game in the shop league. Crossing the main running track and football field to get to the game, Jim spied the varsity team high jumpers practicing leaps over a jump bar.

Jim later said that the jumpers had set the bar higher and higher as they practiced and that when it finally reached five feet nine inches, no one was able to clear it. Jim, who was dressed in his work clothes, spoke up and asked if he could give it a try. The other athletes chuckled at the idea but told him to go ahead. Jim sprinted back and forth a few times to warm up and then took a run for the bar. He rolled right over it, much to the surprise of the athletes standing around him. One of the observers told Pop Warner about Thorpe's feat and suggested him for the track team. In no time, Jim was on the Carlisle squad.

Warner quickly sized up Thorpe's talent for jumping and assigned one of the school's top athletes, Albert Exendine, the task of working with the boy. Jim was no doubt impressed to be paired with Exendine, who was an extremely popular track and football star on campus and a top-ranking student as well. Exendine held the majority of the Carlisle track-and-field records. Thorpe certainly benefited from training with "Ex," for he went on to better all of those records in his first season!

But the biggest benefit of making the track team, for Jim at least, was that the outing program did not apply to athletes. They were allowed to remain on campus during the summer, when Carlisle took on a more relaxed pace, to train for and compete in intercollegiate events. In fact, not long after joining the team, Thorpe gave his first official performance during a meet with Pennsylvania State College. He placed second in the high jump behind another teammate.

Jim achieved athletic recognition at the last regular meet of the season against Bucknell, where he finished second in the 120-yard hurdles. That earned him a varsity letter, and he soon sported an oversize maroon sweater with a giant "C" over his chest. Thorpe topped the season by wowing audiences at the Pennsylvania Junior College Interscholastic Meet. It was here that he surpassed each of Exendine's records.

That kind of reward was just what Jim needed to boost his self-esteem. He remained modest as he enjoyed the clips about him that began to show up in Carlisle's school newspaper. "James Thorpe is working hard to make the football squad," the paper's "Arrowhead" column noted. "If James can equal his track records on the football squad, he will be a star." He didn't have to share much of the limelight with the older stars of the football team, since most of them were playing semiprofessional or minor-league ball for the summer throughout the eastern states. Thorpe looked forward to earning a little baseball money himself the next summer, after he had better established himself as an athlete. He liked baseball enough, in fact, to play just for the fun of it, money or no money. That was one of the things that marked Thorpe as a true sportsman.

Chapter 4

NEWCOMER ON THE GRIDIRON

When Jim Thorpe came out for football practice in the fall, his lithe, narrow-shouldered runner's frame didn't look ready for a football uniform. But Thorpe eagerly donned the shoulder pads and crimson jersey and ran onto the field, where tackling practice was underway. There to meet him were Carlisle's finest football players; compared with them the 155-pounder looked fragile.

Coach Warner was conducting an exercise in which a running back was given the ball and made to run the field until tackled by any one of the squad waiting for him. Warner wasn't sure about Thorpe. Here was one of his top track men, risking himself in some tough maneuvers.

The coach was as surprised as the rest of them when Thorpe's turn came. Jim ran through the entire pack with lightning speed, dodging neatly between would-be tacklers, without being downed. It was no fluke, either, for Thorpe trotted back to the end zone and delivered his performance a second time. Warner recognized the elements of a great running back and knew that if Thorpe were taught how to kick and throw the ball and how to tackle and block, he would become an outstanding player.

Exendine was again entrusted with training Thorpe and some of the other new players. Thorpe was adept at learning by example. And Exendine, who more than once was named to All-American teams by football writer and authority Walter Camp, was a fine example. "Thorpe was a good learner," Exendine later said to Jack Newcombe, author of *The Best of the Athletic Boys.* "He was quick at doing things the way you showed him. He wasn't afraid and I kept at him about being mean when he had the ball or was blocking and tackling."

Thorpe was added immediately to the varsity squad—quite a feat, considering that he was up against top talent trying out for the team. The athlete status had certain advantages, too. To begin with, Thorpe took up residence in the new football quarters, located near the team's Indian Field. These quarters provided a luxurious home in comparison with the regular students' dorms. There were pool tables, a phonograph, and a reading room. Also featured were a dining room and a special kitchen that put out all the food the boys could eat. And the food was far more appetizing than the dull fare Thorpe had been used to.

In return, Jim put in a lot of hours on the practice field, learning the basics of football. He was a fine runner but was raw in other aspects of the sport. For that reason, and because he had to pay his dues in the ranks, Thorpe spent much of the 1907 football season on the bench as a reserve player for Albert Payne. Fortunately for Thorpe, the older left back got into enough scrapes to give Jim some time on the field.

Jim saw his first action during a warm-up preseason game with Lebanon Valley College in September. Thorpe played in the second half, along with several other first-year players, and helped Carlisle win with a score of 40-0. What was to be a historic season for the Carlisle squad got off to a good start with the home opener against Villanova, which also fell to the Indians. Warner, always innovative, had worked closely with the team to create new ways of handling the ball. Early football was mostly a running game; forward passes were not allowed, and the emphasis was placed on scoring with field goals, then worth four points. But the rules recently had been changed to allow some passing, and Warner was first in using unusual combinations of offensive running and passing. The Indians' speed and their willingness to learn contributed to the team's success.

Over the next several weeks, the Carlisle squad smashed through the collegiate ranks. It beat Susquehanna, Pennsylvania State College, Syracuse University, and Bucknell in rapid-fire succession, drawing the attention of the nation. One of the most exciting matches came late in October, when Carlisle visited the University of Pennsylvania, one of the strongest teams in the country.

The Indians played aggressive ball and passed the pigskin

so skillfully that Penn players were often confused as to its whereabouts. The previously undefeated Penn crumpled, losing to Carlisle by a score of 26-6. Said the *New York Times*, "The entire Indian team played magnificent ball," with all the players tackling "like fiends, Penn being unable to gain through their line, around the ends or run back on punts. . . . The Indians just swept them off their feet."

Later in the season, Carlisle went on to beat the eminent Harvard University in Cambridge, Massachusetts—the first time they had defeated Harvard. The Indians also took post-season games with the University of Minnesota and the University of Chicago, thanks to what the *Times* called "clever trick plays and beautifully executed forward passes." The team had racked up a remarkable ten-win, one-loss season, having lost only to Princeton University. And Thorpe, now twenty-one, gained invaluable experience, not only in learning about football strategy and playing skills, but also in traveling with the team.

Jim returned to Carlisle to admiring classmates. The good feelings of success went a long way toward improving his studies, too. He earned better marks in many classes and one day was even trusted by one of his teachers to take over the class while she was absent.

Important to his athletic development was Jim's continuing interest in a variety of sports, including baseball, basketball, football, and track and field. It was his love for sports, as well as a curiosity about and a willingness to try new games, that helped make him an outstanding athlete. Even though football had absorbed him and given him a glimmer of fame, he was still interested in competing in the less glamorous track events in the springtime.

Thorpe began the 1908 track season with a bang, winning the high jump at the Penn relays in Philadelphia and finishing third in his first high hurdles. At a Syracuse, New York, meet in early May, he stunned audiences by taking five first-place awards in hurdles, jumps, and the shot put. As if that weren't enough, he walked away with five top ribbons for his feats in two other regional meets that spring.

After track and field was finished for the spring, Thorpe requested a leave of absence to return home, promising to come back and finish his course of study in the fall. Getting back to Oklahoma, Jim had the opportunity to catch up on family events and visit with friends who had grown up on other farms near the Thorpes'. He also had a chance to relax, to take as much time as he wanted to go hunting with his brother Frank, and to socialize in town. But by the time late August rolled around, Jim was eager to get back to Carlisle and the beginning of football training. He had filled out to 175 pounds, which would only improve his performance on the field.

Thorpe trained diligently for the 1908 football season, working especially on developing his famed placekicking accuracy. Many senior players graduated and it was up to younger players like Thorpe to carry the point-scoring load for Carlisle. His ability to kick field goals from a variety of positions on the field and to kick them consistently became crucial in Carlisle's achieving a ten-win, two-loss, one-tie season.

The efficient team of quarterback Mike Balenti and Thorpe kicked and punted their way through games that otherwise might have been lost to some fine opponents. Balenti, one of Carlisle's best students, had served as a model for Thorpe when the younger player was learning to kick the ball. The smaller of the two, Balenti would single-handedly score all sixteen points during a shutout victory over Navy later in the season, entirely by kicking field goals.

The Carlisle team staged shutout games against its first three warm-up opponents of the season before getting down to business with Penn State in early October. Thorpe kicked three spectacular field goals. Each one was executed with grace and speed. The score was a victory for the Indians at 12-6. Carlisle went on to smash Syracuse with a 12-0 score the next week. Said the *New York Times* of the team's brightest prospect, "Carlisle depended upon Thorpe for her scorings. He made three pretty goals. . . . The game was a very open one, the Indians resorting to many startling trick plays that netted never less than twenty yards."

But the game of the season, as far as Thorpe was concerned, was the October 24, 1908, game against Pennsylvania, which Thorpe later spoke of as the hardest game he had ever played. Both teams came into the match undefeated. The Indians and the Quakers were so well matched, in fact, that the teams played to a 6-6 tie. Thorpe was frustrated throughout the game in his attempts to kick a field goal, but he proved his worth as a running back.

According to the *Times*, "In the second half Balenti and Thorpe were the stars in the making of the Indian touchdown. Balenti ran back one of Hollenback's punts for twenty-five yards to the Quakers' forty-yard line. On the next play, Thorpe worked his way through the Quaker forwards and without interference started for the Quaker goal." Fleet as a deer, Thorpe ran sixty yards before a Quaker tackle caught up with him at the five-yard line. "Thorpe literally threw himself over the line for the touchdown [worth five points then] and then kicked a very difficult goal, tying the score."

The Indians went on to crush the undefeated Navy team, 16-6, thanks to Balenti's incredible field-goal kicking. Carlisle was at last brought down by Harvard, 17-0, but completed the last five games of the season with four additional victories. That season, the Indians outscored their opponents by a fantastic margin—212 to 55 points. Thorpe's mighty kicking toe caught national attention, and Jim was named to Walter Camp's third-pick All-America team.

Thorpe met with more success, again proving his versatility, during the 1909 track and field season the following spring. He won strings of gold medals against a variety of colleges. Against Lafayette alone, Thorpe won six gold medals and a bronze! The athletic powerhouse won first in the high jump, his best event, and in the broad jump, shot put, discus throw, 120-yard high hurdles, and 220-yard low hurdles. Before the season was over, Thorpe won fourteen more gold medals and two silver ones, establishing himself as one of the top track talents in the nation. It was a reputation he was to keep.

When summer vacation came, Jim wasn't keen on going back to Oklahoma. So he tagged along with some friends on Carlisle's sports teams who were going to North Carolina to play summer baseball. Many of the college athletes went out of town to play minor-league baseball for the summer. Managers of small clubs were anxious to sign on students because they played relatively well at fairly low prices. When Jim arrived in Rocky Mount, North Carolina, he found a team in the East Carolina League that was willing to pay him fifteen dollars a week to play a base. It wasn't much money, even by the day's standard, but was enough to cover his living expenses while away from Carlisle.

Jim loved baseball enough to forget the low pay and played throughout the summer of 1909 for Rocky Mount in towns situated up and down the Atlantic Coast Line Railway. He was given the opportunity to pitch and did well, considering his inexperience at pro ball, winning nine games and losing ten for the season. He boasted a .253 batting average, helped by rapid-fire runs to bases that kept the infielders scrambling to tag him.

Jim Thorpe took great pleasure in the towns' baseball fans, especially the kids. He would let them carry his baseball glove, shoes, or a bat, joke with them, and make them feel special. With his friends, he was a jovial companion and loved to go out at night for entertainment—sometimes, it has been said, a little too much entertainment at the local taverns.

The whole baseball experience was so pleasant that Thorpe decided not to return to Carlisle in the fall. He was back on the Rocky Mount field the next season, in 1910, after a return to Oklahoma during the fall and winter. When the baseball work dried up, Thorpe stayed on in Oklahoma as a guest of relatives and worked as a hired hand where needed.

At Carlisle, meanwhile, Pop Warner was having a tough time getting his team to perform as they had during the past couple of years. The 1910 season brought eight wins, but six losses, and Warner sorely missed the talents of Thorpe. Luckily for Pop, the former Carlisle quarterback, Albert Exendine, bumped into Thorpe on the streets of Anadarko, Oklahoma, during the summer of 1911. Thorpe was pleased to see his old mentor and asked Albert how things were back East. Ex was surprised at how much his twenty-four-year-old friend had grown since he had seen him last—Thorpe now stood six feet tall and weighed almost two hundred pounds. Ex told Jim how much Warner needed him.

At Ex's urging, Thorpe wired Carlisle, asking if he could be readmitted. Warner was enthusiastic about his coming back and reminded Thorpe that, with the 1912 Olympics coming up, there would be no better place to train for the United States team tryouts than Carlisle. By September, Thorpe was on the train for Pennsylvania heading for the comforts of the football boys' quarters that he had left two years earlier. He had just gotten settled when the football season of 1911 started. The traditional warm-up games against smaller Pennsylvania colleges kicked off what was to be a stellar year for Carlisle's team.

As in previous years, the smaller colleges provided practice for the Carlisle reserve team early in the season. The first five games of the season, in fact, went fairly easily. The first big challenger was the University of Pittsburgh. It was Thorpe's day and he dominated the game with his skillful kicking, using it throughout the game as an offensive tactic. On punts, Thorpe kicked the ball so high in the air and ran so fast that he often beat the ball down the field. He was there, ready to battle the opposition for the ball, and sometimes grabbed it and dashed off for the goal line. The *Pittsburgh Leader* was particularly impressed with Carlisle's 17-0 victory and wrote:

To say Thorpe is the whole team would be fifty

percent wrong, but he certainly is the most consistent performer trotted out on the [Pittsburgh] gridiron in many a moon. His returning of punts, line-bucking, fake plays, and other maneuvers got him great applause. Thorpe carried the ball two out of every three times for the visitors.

The other Pittsburgh paper, the *Dispatch*, seemed to want to top such praise with its own glowing account:

This person Thorpe was a host in himself. Tall and sinewy, as quick as a flash and as powerful as a turbine engine, he appeared to be impervious to injury. Kicking from 50 to 70 yards every time his shoe crashed against the ball, he seemed possessed of super-human speed, for wherever the pigskin alighted, there he was, ready either to grab it or to down the Pitt player who secured it. At line-bucking and general all-around work, this Sac and Fox shone resplendent and then some.

Against Pennsylvania two weeks later, Carlisle continued to rout the opposition, in spite of Thorpe's absence. He had suffered a painful twisted ankle the week before in a successful game with Lafayette and had been benched by Pop

Warner for two weeks so the ankle could heal. The rest of the team proved that, even without Thorpe, they were stronger and faster than the highly rated Penn.

But by November 11, 1911, Thorpe was feeling ready to take on the defending national champion, Harvard University. Sports fans all over the country were geared up for the game; descriptions of Thorpe and his triumphs had been splashed across newspapers coast to coast. Some thirty thousand fans turned out in Cambridge, Massachusetts, to see Thorpe and the Carlisle eleven live up to the stories. Thorpe's ankle was still tender from his injury and he was not expected to dominate the game. So confident of a victory was the Harvard coach that he didn't even attend the game. He left the coaching in the hands of an assistant and left orders to play only the reserve team so that the varsity team would be fresh for later games.

During the first half, though Thorpe had scored field goals in both periods (then worth 3 points), Harvard led 9-6. Caught up in the need for more points, Thorpe forgot about his bandaged leg. The *New York Times* observed:

> ... The Indians came back strong in the third period and with a touchdown and goal and another goal from the field by Thorpe, Harvard was left behind 15 to 9, before the regulars came onto the gridiron for the last quarter.

The captain of the Harvard team, dismayed by the score, disregarded the coach's orders and led the varsity players, spanking fresh, onto the field. It looked as if the weary Indians, who never traveled with many substitute players, might be in trouble. But the Harvard effort came too late. Thorpe kicked one more magnificent field goal forty-eight yards from the post. The Indians held Harvard to scoring just one touchdown before time ran out with the score 18-15 in Carlisle's favor.

Thorpe's ankle finally caused him to collapse and, as he was helped off the field, an ovation roared out from the stands. The Boston papers added their praise the next day:

> Even the most partisan Crimson [Harvard] supporter will gladly admit, through their admiration for his wonderful work against Harvard, that [Thorpe] not only upheld an already great reputation, but that he has placed his name in the Hall of Fame, not only of Carlisle but also of the entire football world. It was indeed a pleasure to see a man not only live up to a great reputation but add to it through work beautifully accomplished.

Coming down from the high of their Harvard victory, the Indians were defeated the following Saturday at Syracuse in New York State. Thanks to a recent snowstorm, the playing field was a pool of mud and slush, making Thorpe's kicking game difficult. Also Gus Welch, the Indians' crack quarterback and Thorpe's best friend, was out with a sore back. The Syracuse team had spent all week psyching themselves up to beat the undefeated Carlisle. And they did—by one point, 12-11.

Carlisle finished the remaining two games of the season with victories, however. In the final game, against Brown University in Rhode Island, the entire team played well. Welch made a fantastic sixty-two-yard run for a touchdown; Thorpe kicked twenty-seven- and thirty-three-yard field goals and, despite the muddy conditions, made a breathtaking eighty-three-yard punt. It set a new collegiate record.

Returning to Carlisle was certainly a happy occasion for the Indians' football team. So high was their respect for him that the team elected Thorpe their captain. Jim garnered respect from other circles, too. He had met a senior-class girl named Iva Miller, a Scots-Irish Cherokee from Oklahoma, and was her date at the Pennsylvania-game dance during the fall. Though she was only eighteen (to Jim's twenty-four), she was one of her class's best students and was due to graduate in a few months. The two became an item around campus that winter. For the first time since parting with his family, Jim enjoyed warm feelings of affection and sensed that he had found a new home.

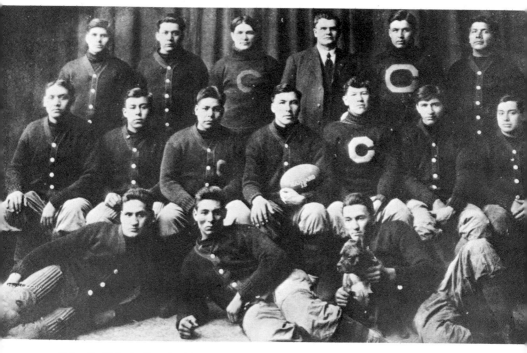

The Carlisle Indian football team of 1911 with Coach Pop Warner standing in the last row. Jim Thorpe, with the Carlisle letter sweater, is seated in front of the coach.

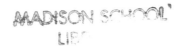

Pop Warner and Jim Thorpe

Jim Thorpe playing for the New York Giants

Jim Thorpe and his daughter Grace

In September, 1948, Jim Thorpe, at the age of sixty-one, gave a dropkicking
exhibition at New York's Polo Grounds.

Jim Thorpe's children received replicas of their father's medals in January, 1983. Left to right: William, Charlotte, Gail, International Olympic Committee President Juan Samaranch (shaking hands with Charlotte), Richard, Grace, and John.

In 1984 the United States issued a stamp honoring Jim Thorpe.
The stamp shows Jim Thorpe in his football uniform of
Carlisle.

Bill Thorpe, Jr., and Gina Hemphill, grandchildren of Olympic champions Jim Thorpe and Jesse Owens, received the Olympic torch when it arrived in New York for the 1984 Olympic games in Los Angeles.

Chapter 5

RIGHT LIVING AND RIGHT THINKING

One of the biggest amusements for Carlisle students during the winter of early 1912 was a visit to the school gymnasium. There, Pop Warner could be found pushing Jim Thorpe and Louis Tewanima to their limits. The two were in training for the U.S. Olympic team tryouts, and all the school's hopes for sending a representative to the 1912 games in Stockholm, Sweden, rested on the two athletes' shoulders. Of course, the best training of all would be actual competition, and Warner could hardly wait to enter both boys in the spring track season events.

And what a season it was! Thorpe swept nearly every competition he entered and Tewanima, a Hopi Indian of slight build who specialized in distance running, won most of his events. During the spring, Thorpe won eleven gold medals for first-place wins, four silver medals, and three bronze. It wasn't unusual for him to place first in four, five, or six events in the same meet. Events that he frequently won included the 100-yard dash; the 45-, 120-, and 220-yard hurdles; the standing, broad, and high jumps; and the shot put, both twelve and sixteen pounds.

Just one example of his prowess came at a track meet with

Carlisle, the University of Pennsylvania, and Carnegie Technical School. Thorpe was "the star of the meet," the newspaper account said. He won the high jump, the shot put, and the 220-yard hurdles; he was second in the broad jump and the 120-yard hurdles; and he was third in the 100-yard dash—all in one day. The only event in which he failed to score was the hammer throw. Carlisle walked off with eighty-two points in the meet, as compared with thirty-two for both the other teams combined.

Thorpe and Tewanima both qualified for the Olympics in tryouts that spring. For Thorpe, then twenty-five, the trip to Sweden with the United States team was the most exciting and exhilarating part of his Olympic experience. "I'd never seen a boat as big as that before," he later recalled. "I've seen a lot since. But nothing was like that—walking on the boat, and all those cabins and the decks and eating and sleeping on it."

The team departed from New York City on June 14, 1912, aboard the S.S. *Finland*, specially commissioned to make the trip to Stockholm. The send-off itself was a festive occasion. About five thousand well-wishers were on hand to bid farewell to the athletes, each of them waving an American flag and cheering loudly. The *Finland*, too, was decked out in red, white, and blue, and the scene was vivid with color. Just before the ship steamed out at nine in the morning, a crowd of two hundred members of local athletic clubs and organizations showed up on the dock led by a costumed Uncle Sam. Each carried a flag and around each stick was wrapped a ribbon with the message, "Bring Home the Bacon."

The team included athletes from colleges and athletic clubs around the country, and was regarded by experts as the finest group of United States athletes ever assembled. Their voyage was not to be a pleasure cruise; it was treated as a training mission. A cork track one-eighth of a mile long was laid out on the deck. Mats were set out for high jumping and vaulting practice, and a special pool had been constructed for swimmers. An entire dining cabin was set aside especially for the athletes, 150 in number, so that their meals could be supervised by the team trainers. Despite stories that Thorpe didn't train during the voyage, his teammates recalled that he worked diligently during each of the team's daily workouts.

By the time the *Finland* arrived in Stockholm ten days later, the team was anxious to participate, to say the least. The combined antics of 150 "jocks" proved to be a bit much for the confines of a ship, as the *New York Times* reported. It was a rowdy boat trip, with "several cases of insubordination" noted. "Three athletes behaved so badly that they had to be warned by the *Finland*'s officers." The *Times* concluded by saying that forty men had practically broken training, but declined to offer details.

Upon arriving in Stockholm, the Americans were met by

another highly enthusiastic crowd. Among the welcomers were members of the Swedish Olympic Committee and its entire track team, which sang both Swedish and American songs as the ship docked. The American athletes soon became one of the biggest attractions of the Olympics. They were one of the largest teams, and probably the most extroverted, to visit the city.

The *Times* described the atmosphere of Stockholm in the early summer:

> Stockholm presents a festive appearance. The streets are decorated with thousands of Swedish flags, blue with a yellow cross, on poles planted a hundred feet apart. The flags of other nationalities represented at the Olympic games are interspersed in profusion. The contestants from the various countries, all wearing distinctive uniforms, and easily recognized by national devices on their hat bands, are seen everywhere. Between 2,000 and 3,000 of them have arrived here. . . . The weather, as in 1908, favors the Americans, who are more accustomed to heat than their British rivals. The thermometer for the past four days has stood at about 90 degrees.

As with every Olympics, the games began with a stirring

parade of athletes through the brand-new stadium. Teams with flags from twenty-eight countries made the circuit around the running track, representing 3,889 competitors. The facilities were the pride of Sweden. A special seating box was set aside for King Gustav V and Crown Prince Gustav Adolph of Sweden and Grand Duke Dimitri of Russia, who witnessed the ceremonies.

The next day was Jim Thorpe's first in the games. Competition in the pentathlon began with the broad jump. In photographs one can see the perfect form Thorpe showed in his jump. His arms were high in the air and his legs curled beneath him at a right angle to his body. He sailed 23 feet 2.7 inches, which beat the rest of the contenders. He didn't throw the javelin quite as successfully, placing third with a throw of just under 153 feet 3 inches, as compared with the winner's mark of 162 feet 7 inches.

Failing to take first place in that event may have been what compelled Jim to outperform his competitors in the remaining three events. He hurled the discus 116 feet 8.4 inches, three feet farther than his United States teammate, Avery Brundage. He edged out two other Americans in the 200-meter dash, his teammates behind his 22.9 seconds by a tenth of a second. And he stunned spectators with a wide-lead finish in the 1,500-meter race, clocking a time of 4 minutes 44.8 seconds and leaving the others many feet behind.

European observers were amazed, of course, that world-class athletes from their continent did not win, and even United States officials were pleasantly surprised. "Although we expected that Thorpe would win the pentathlon, his great performance exceeded our hopes," said a member of the United States Olympic Committee that afternoon.

Thorpe had plenty of time to get in condition for the next event he was entered in, the decathlon. Competition, which was spread over three days, started the following week, so Thorpe had time to train aboard the ship and watch his fellow teammates dominate the games. Each weekday various heats in the running competition were held. Time and again, the United States athletes scored gold. They took the silver and bronze medals, too, in the 100-meter dash. Americans scooped up both first- and third-place wins in the 400-meter race, and took a first in the 3,000-meter relays, the gold and silver in the standing high jump, first and third in the hammer throw, third in the marathon, and many more medals during the week.

The track events were all held in the stadium, sometimes simultaneously, and often were confusing to watch. "The exhibition in the stadium is as hard for a spectator to follow as a three-ring circus," one correspondent noted. "There was something doing on the cinder track most of the time to-day and within the oval the jumping and pentathlon events took place." Among the competitors in this jumble of events was

Louis Tewanima, who won a silver medal in the 10,000-meter race.

While waiting for their events to come up, Thorpe and other athletes found plenty to see and do when they weren't training. Philip Noel-Baker, an English athlete, wrote:

> We found that Stockholm had a powerful attraction that was all its own—grass and roses at almost every turn; the lovely waterfront, bathed, as I remember, every day in the glittering sun; the Royal Palaces . . . and not least the forest, then close around the city, where we went in the evenings to dance with sedate but friendly and very pretty Swedish girls. Everyone in Stockholm was eager to give us help.

When Saturday finally came, Thorpe started competition in the decathlon, which began with the 100-meter dash, the running broad jump, and the shot put. It was raining on and off, just enough to make conditions slippery and difficult for the athletes. Jim was beaten in the 100-meter dash, coming in third, and was second in the running broad jump. In the third event, he finally achieved a first, heaving the shot 42 feet 5.5 inches, more than two feet farther than the second-place effort. Thorpe closed out the day with a slight lead.

Weather was perfect the next day as decathlon competition continued with the running high jump, the 110-meter hurdles, and the 400-meter run. Thorpe was particularly adept at the first two events, and he easily took a first in the high jump competition with a height of 6 feet 1.6 inches. Jim would never really be interested in setting records, though he held a few in his time. Rather, he simply wanted to win the event or game at hand. His high jump was good enough to win the event; yet he had jumped a much more spectacular 6 feet 5 inches while training for the games.

Thorpe ended up in fourth place in the 400-meter race but turned in another first-place performance—and a new record—in the 110-meter hurdles. His time of 15.6 seconds would stand as a record for many years. Coming out of the second day of competition, Thorpe still maintained his lead. Only one day remained, not only for the decathlon but for all the games. Gold medals would be awarded for all winners at the close of the games, and Stockholm was buzzing in anticipation of the finale.

Jim Thorpe hadn't had much experience or training at Carlisle for events other than jumping and running. But he was always ready and able to learn by imitation. So Coach Warner probably wasn't too surprised, although immensely pleased, to see Thorpe take second place in the discus throw, third place in the javelin throw, and third place in the pole vault. It was in the final event of the day that Jim shone, however. Despite fatigue from exerting himself in the other events, Thorpe ran the 1,500-meter race in 4 minutes 40.1

seconds, bettering his own record. It remained an impressive performance. Even forty years later, during the 1952 Olympic games, decathlon champion Bob Mathias took ten seconds longer to cross the line!

Thorpe finished with an incredible 8,412.96 points out of a possible 10,000. The nearest competitor, Hugo Wieslander of Sweden, scored almost 700 fewer, with 7,724.5 points. Thorpe's record would not be beaten in Olympic competition until 1926.

Sweden's King Gustav distributed the gold medals during the closing ceremonies, and Thorpe went up twice before the reviewing stand for his pentathlon and decathlon medals. The huge audience gave him a thundering ovation each time. The king, dressed formally in a gray frock coat and silk hat, crowned each medalist with a traditional laurel wreath and placed the medal around his neck. To the king's amusement, some of the athletes found the crown uncomfortable, especially a California boy who, said a correspondent, "looked like a blushing schoolgirl in his wreath." Finally Gustav shook Thorpe's hand in a solemn manner and uttered the famous compliment, "Sir, you are the greatest athlete in the world." Thorpe, almost speechless with modesty, is said to have blurted out, "Thanks, King."

Jim received not only his two gold medals, but glittering trophies as well. A fantastic, four-foot bronze bust in Gustav's likeness was the prize for the pentathlon. For his decathlon feat, Thorpe received an ornate, thirty-pound silver chalice. Given by the tsar of Russia, the jewel-studded cup measured some two feet long and resembled an ancient Viking ship. Thorpe's teammates were also rewarded handsomely. In fact, the American team took home most of the gold medals. In track-and-field events, the United States team had won 85 points, as compared with 24 for Sweden and 14 for Great Britain, the runners-up. In all events, which included sports on horseback, shooting, and boating, the United States still dominated with 128 total points, as compared with the others' 104 and 66 points, respectively.

Ironically, the pentathlon and decathlon events had been added to the Swedish Olympics at the suggestion of athletic experts who wanted a test of all-around talent. The Americans were often charged with specializing in one or two disciplines and not becoming well-rounded athletes. These new events would surely point out the Americans' faults, it was reasoned. Yet it was a full-blooded American, Thorpe, who won the honors in both events. The rest of the world soon learned of his feat and joined in King Gustav's conclusion that Thorpe was a virtual superathlete.

Chapter 6

A HERO COMES HOME

"Thorpe Is The World's Greatest Athlete," read the headline of a story in the *New York Times* shortly after the 1912 Olympics. It was one of dozens of articles that appeared in papers all around the country. Each one echoed the statements of King Gustav of Sweden and of athletic experts. The *Times* continued:

> . . . Probably no athlete who ever lived can boast of such all-around excellence in track and field work as well as in many other lines of physical endeavor. . . . In addition, he is a specialist, and probably the greatest in the world, at football. He runs, side-steps, plunges, dodges as well as the best football player that probably ever lived. He punts and kicks goals with strength and precision, interferes or follows interference with cunning, throws forward passes, and makes inside kicks with the greatest veterans, and tackles and uses the stiff arm with almost perfect technique.

A few days after the article appeared, even the president

of the United States voiced his agreement. In a letter for Thorpe sent to Carlisle, President William Taft wrote:

> I have much pleasure in congratulating you on account of your noteworthy victory at the Olympic Games in Stockholm. Your performance is one of which you may well be proud. You have set a high standard of physical development which is only attained by right living and right thinking, and your victory will serve as an incentive to all to improve these qualities which characterize the best type of American citizen.

When Thorpe, Tewanima, and Pop Warner arrived at Carlisle after their return voyage, they received a jubilant welcome party. The threesome was escorted through the town's streets on a horse carriage, followed by students marching in their military uniforms, local fire departments, and other groups. The parade led to an athletic field where the school superintendent read, with great pomp, a prepared speech. A local baseball game followed, along with dinner at the Elks Club. The two students were then escorted by schoolmates to a gigantic dance on campus. Thorpe and his friends "let loose" and danced until morning.

The crowds in Carlisle's celebration were miniscule as compared with the ones that turned out in New York City the following week. The entire United States Olympic team rode down Fifth Avenue in a motorcade seen by more than a million people. Thorpe, who was seated in a car by himself, had never in his life been thrust before such a throng, and he was overcome with the wonder of it. Other welcomes were held in Boston and Philadelphia. In the latter city, Thorpe and Tewanima were honored, along with other Pennsylvania Olympic competitors, and enjoyed a banquet with baseball hero Ty Cobb.

Naturally, there were plenty of businessmen eager to cash in on all of Thorpe's newfound world fame. He received an offer to join a traveling show as well as several offers to join professional baseball teams. But Thorpe was advised to return to Carlisle for one more season. Pop Warner argued that he could finish his certificate of learning, while at the same time gain further attention as a football player and become more valuable to professional clubs. So Thorpe settled back into the comforts of the athletic quarters at Carlisle, surrounded once again by admiring fellow athletes and students. At twenty-five, he was in peak condition and was poised for a brilliant, final season of collegiate football.

The first games of the season, as always, were warm-up games played against smaller schools. All four competitors suffered shutouts at the hands of the Indians, whose swift, precise ball handling and clever strategy far outclassed the smaller school teams. Though, for the most part, Warner played Carlisle's substitute team during the games, Thorpe and the varsity regulars did see some action. Thorpe thrilled the crowds who had come to see their Olympic hero in the Villanova game. He contributed to the 65-0 rout with three touchdowns, made within twenty minutes. As Thorpe left the field after the game, he was caught up in a press of fans, both children and adults. Such close contact with fans was a new experience for him, but one that would soon become familiar.

The Indians did not find it as easy to beat Washington and Jefferson, their next opponent. A huge crowd of ten thousand people had gathered for the game. But Carlisle could not seem to make connections that day; Thorpe himself missed several field-goal attempts, usually simple work for him. At least his desperate fourth-down punts and a string of interceptions held Washington and Jefferson to a 0-0 tie. It was a frustrating afternoon for both teams, as well as for the spectators.

Perhaps that frustration added fuel to the Carlisle team's desire to beat Syracuse the following weekend. Syracuse had beaten the Indians on a rainy day the previous year, keeping them from attaining a perfect season. The Carlisle team was determined not to let that happen again and, despite another rain-soaked field, beat the Syracuse Orangemen 33-0. Warner had Thorpe run straight through the scrimmage line with the ball instead of making his usual crafty runs around the ends. The tactic was highly successful. Thorpe scored three touchdowns during the game and, in spite of the soggy conditions, demonstrated some excellent kicking.

Thorpe played just as brilliantly under pressure at the Pittsburgh game that followed and throughout the rest of the season. Pitt was defeated 45-8, with Carlisle scoring in all four periods of play. That game was followed by a victory over Georgetown University, 34-20, and the chance to play a Canadian rugby team from the University of Toronto. The game with Toronto was played under American football rules in the first half and then under rules for the closely related rugby style of play in the second half. Carlisle played expertly under both sets of rules. One Toronto paper said of Thorpe, "He had everything, including speed, strength, and ability to punt, drop, place, pass, catch and tackle, beside displaying remarkable coolness and the best of judgment."

Carlisle went on to blitz Lehigh 34-14, with Thorpe scoring 28 points himself. One spectacular touchdown was gained when Thorpe intercepted a Lehigh pass right in the opponent's end zone. Instead of grounding the ball, Thorpe decided to run with it, even though the Lehigh team was swamping him. Pop Warner must have dropped his cigar at the sidelines. Thorpe dodged the entire throng, somehow made his way out of the end zone, and galloped 110 yards for a goal. It seemed amazing that Thorpe could be such a proficient kicker of punts and field goals, yet also be the best running back in the country. He added new meaning to the term "versatile." As a result, Thorpe often appeared in almost every play in a game, regardless of whether the ball was being passed or run up the field.

The entire team was keyed up for the game against Army at West Point Academy on November 9, 1912. The Army team's players were much bigger, on the average, than the Indians. But the Indians were faster. Pop Warner was anxious to prove to skeptics that Carlisle could take on even the toughest of opponents and beat them by sheer speed and agility. Thorpe didn't score any of the touchdowns but helped to set them up for teammates Alex Arcasa and Joe Bergie. He did return a punt for forty-five yards, running wildly through the entire Army team for a touchdown, only to have it scratched because of an offsides penalty. The *New York Times* liked the play nonetheless, calling it a run that "will go down in the Army gridiron annals as one of the greatest ever seen on the plains."

One of the halfbacks playing against Carlisle—and getting almost nowhere in trying to stop Thorpe's and Arcasa's swift, crisscross runs—was West Point cadet Dwight Eisenhower, who of course went on to become a five-star general and president of the United States. Every time "Ike" tried to stop Thorpe, he was bowled over. Ike would later say that Thorpe was the best football player he had ever seen.

Just as in the previous season, the Indians went from an astounding victory streak to a disappointing loss. Syracuse had kept the Carlisle team from a non-loss season the year before; Pennsylvania checked the Indians during the 1912 season. The team seemed tired and careless on the field and lost because of several fumbles, missed goal attempts, and lackluster blocking. Thorpe certainly tried hard to run the ball and on one play tore off an exciting 80-yard sprint for a touchdown. There were many more exciting runs, but not enough to push the Carlisle score higher. The Indians lost 34-26. Ironically, they had gained almost 400 yards during the game, far superior to Penn's 177 yards.

The last big game of the season would be the traditional Thanksgiving Day game at Brown University in Providence, Rhode Island. To give the team a workout between the Penn and Brown games, Warner agreed to a game with the Springfield (Massachusetts) Training School, which was the nation's original YMCA organization. The Springfield team gave the Indians a tough challenge, but Thorpe electrified the audience with a strong performance. Said the *New York Times*:

> Thorpe made four touchdowns and kicked three goals from the field and one from placement. . . . The third period was Thorpe's inning. The Indian sprinted 57 yards before being tackled,

the star run of the game. He showed wonderful work in a broken field. . . . Thorpe plunged through the Y.M.C.A. line for [another] touchdown, scattering the opposing players as though they were mere chips. With graceful ease and unerring accuracy he kicked the goal. At the close of the third period the score stood: Carlisle, 27; Y.M.C.A., 14.

The Indians stayed on at Worcester, Massachusetts, for a few days of training before moving on. During a workout one day, a crowd of football fans and members of the press dropped by to watch the action. One of them was reporter Roy Johnson of the *Worcester Telegram*, who was chatting on the sidelines with Charley Clancy, a baseball manager from a nearby town. When Thorpe passed by on the field, Clancy spotted him and said to Johnson, "I know that guy!" Clancy had been a manager of the Fayetteville, North Carolina, ball club that had picked up Thorpe as a pitcher in a trade with the Rocky Mount club two years earlier.

That normally wouldn't have been big news. After all, a lot of college athletes played summer baseball for money. Technically, however, it was considered professional ball playing. Since professionalism could ruin an athlete's amateur standing and keep him from playing college sports, most of the boys played under fake names. Thorpe did not because when he had left Carlisle, he hadn't decided if he were ever going back. As far as he was concerned, he might become a major league baseball player if he were discovered by a talent scout while playing in the East Carolina League.

But it was big news, indeed, to Johnson, who realized that he had a hot story on his hands. Thorpe, a national hero, had won his Olympic medals while a professional, not an amateur. He had "tainted" his pure athletic standing by playing baseball for a few dollars a week. Had Thorpe been anyone less famous, Johnson wouldn't have bothered to print a story about it. As it was, he took two months to decide whether he should go with the story and expose Thorpe's past.

In the meantime, Thorpe announced to Johnson and the other reporters that he would soon be leaving Carlisle. The *New York Times* reported:

> Jim Thorpe, the famous Indian athlete, held the limelight to-day, and gave out the statement, following the practice of the Carlisle team, that he intended to sever his connection with the Indian school after the Brown game Thanksgiving Day. The only reason Thorpe gives for quitting the Indian school is that of an absolute dislike of notoriety and utter abhorrence of the public gaze, which his athletic prowess has brought him.

Because he would soon leave school and decide on the best way to market himself as a professional, Thorpe realized that the Brown game would be a milestone for him. It would be his last competition as an amateur, he thought, as well as his last game for Pop Warner. And it would be the last game he would ever play for Carlisle, where he had first run onto the gridiron five years before. He had made some close friends on the team, and knew it would be difficult to leave. Thorpe was determined to make the Brown game a lasting tribute to Warner, his teammates, and himself.

He had to fight a swirling snowstorm to do it. When the Indians and their player-captain, Thorpe, trotted onto the field at Providence the next weekend, a heavy snow was coming down, making the eight thousand spectators edgy. Gus Welch was out of the game with an injury, so it was Alex Arcasa as quarterback who set the pace of the game with Thorpe. They gave Brown the famous Carlisle one-two: a quick rush down the middle of the scrimmage line for one or two downs to gain some yardage and then a swift run by Thorpe around right. Another run might follow, left or end, for another first down or, when a hole in the defense was found, there would be a dash for big yardage or a touchdown. Noted the *Providence Journal*:

> The Redskins had a finely developed interference for their big star, but time and time again

Thorpe broke away from it, doubled back on his trail and was off through open territory on a lope that looked slow, but which in reality was fast running and baffled the tacklers. He eluded the outstretched arms of the tacklers with ridiculous ease, giving the finest exhibition of dodging ever shown on the field.

Thorpe's runs were all of substantial yardage and contributed each time to a score or a first down. In the first period, he blazed past scrimmage with two runs of twenty and thirty yards each. In the second, Carlisle scored two touchdowns, one after Thorpe's thirty-three-yard dash and the other by Jim himself on a fifty-yard run. Closing out the fourth period were two more touchdowns by Thorpe. For one, he tore off a fifty-yard run on a punt return. The other came after runs by Bergie and Wheelock and a piercing, twenty-two-yard Thorpe pass.

The *Journal* praised Thorpe's passing, too, along with his defensive ability:

His great strength on defense was strikingly evident in the second period in particular when Brown, making her greatest bid for a touchdown, had the ball inside Carlisle's five-yard line. Twice Tenney, a 192-pound back, hurled himself into the line and each time Thorpe caught him in mid-air, and without giving ground an inch, . . . hurled him back four yards.

Thorpe's last touchdown, which put the score at Carlisle 32, Brown 0, was significant. Not only was it his last goal in collegiate football, but it was his twenty-fifth touchdown of the season. He had tallied an astronomical 198 points. Jim didn't know it at the time, nor did the people quitting the stadium to escape the snow, but he had just set an all-time college record for a season point total. To top it off, Walter Camp, football expert, selected Thorpe as All-American half-back, first team, for the second year in a row. The *New York Herald* concluded the season with this: "Summing everything up, Jim Thorpe appears to have possessed about every quality necessary to make a player close to perfection."

Thorpe was given a few weeks' vacation to return to his Oklahoma home, his first trip there since winning Olympic honors. He visited with brother Frank and sister Mary, as well as with other relatives near Shawnee, and enjoyed a quiet Christmas season. He returned to Carlisle in January, in time for an annual school reception and dance in the gym. Thorpe seemed to excel at everything he tried—he even won a cake for doing the best two-step. That prize quickly disappeared, consumed by Thorpe and his buddies in the football quarters. In a matter of days, Thorpe was to lose some much bigger prizes.

Chapter 7

"A MOST UNPLEASANT AFFAIR"

Less than a week after Jim Thorpe returned to Carlisle from his Oklahoma holiday in January of 1913, a sensational story about him appeared in the *Worcester Telegram*. It was written by Roy Johnson, the reporter who had seen Thorpe just before Thanksgiving in Springfield, Massachusetts. The story gave details of Thorpe's minor-league baseball experience of 1909-1910, as related to the reporter in a conversation with Charles Clancy, the former baseball manager from North Carolina.

By the next day, James Sullivan, chairman of the Registration Committee of the Amateur Athletic Union, to which Thorpe belonged, was calling for a January 27 hearing by the AAU board to discuss the charges of professionalism. "If he is found to have broken the rules, as stated," Sullivan told the press, "he will be stripped of all his records, his name taken from the athletic annuals, and he will be compelled to return all the prizes he has won since his infraction of the rules."

Pop Warner was ordered by Sullivan to appear before the board with any evidence he might have about Thorpe's recent past. Three days before the meeting, Warner told the press that Clancy had written him, saying, "I never made the statement that I signed Thorpe to pitch for my club, nor did I in any way question his amateur standing." Clancy even denied that Thorpe had ever played ball for him, though indeed he had. Warner joined in the cover-up by telling the papers that Clancy's letter and various rumors were all he had heard about the matter and that there didn't seem to be anything to the story. In reality, Warner had been fully aware that Thorpe and a few of his other football players were off to play baseball, as was the custom, and hadn't done anything to stop them at the time.

The day before the hearing, however, the accusations became more convincing. Two southern ball-players stepped forward and told the press that they had played with Thorpe on the Rocky Mount, North Carolina, baseball team and knew him both by name and appearance. One, Peter Boyle, even quoted Thorpe's complete pitching, batting, and fielding averages for the two years in the league. The headlines in the *New York Times* of January 28 broke the news to the nation: "Olympic Prizes Lost; Thorpe No Amateur; Didn't Realize His Deceit."

Warner and Carlisle Superintendent Moses Friedman, the man who discharged Thorpe in the summer of 1909 to play baseball, both urged Jim to write a letter of "confession" for Warner to present to the AAU. It wasn't really a confession since Thorpe had never hidden the fact in the first place. Nonetheless, the papers and the AAU said Thorpe had committed a deception. The papers printed his so-called confession to Chairman Sullivan in full. It read, in part:

> I played baseball at Rocky Mount and Fayette-ville, N.C., in the summers of 1909 and 1910 under my own name. On the same teams I played with were several college men from the North who were earning money by ball playing during their vacations and who were regarded as amateurs at home. I did not play for the money there was in it because my property brings me in enough money to live on, but because I liked to play ball. I was not very wise to the ways of the world and did not realize that this was wrong and it would make me a profes-sional in track sports. . . .

Thorpe apologized for having kept his ball playing a secret—a gesture probably recommended by Warner and Friedman—and asked for a measure of forgiveness.

> I hope I will be partly excused by the fact that I was simply an Indian schoolboy and did not know all about such things. . . . I have always liked sport and only played or run races for the fun of the thing, and never to earn money. . . . I

hope the Amateur Athletic Union and the people will not be too hard in judging me.

The people weren't hard in their judging, but the AAU was. It was embarrassed to have such blatant professionalism charges brought up in papers around the world and worried that American athletic officials and athletes would come under even more fire. So the AAU decided to make an example of the Thorpe case and prove to the world that it was not about to show any compassion just because Thorpe was an Olympic gold medalist. The United States Olympic Committee, which included AAU officials, said it had sent Thorpe to the Olympics

> . . . without the least suspicion as to there having ever been any act of professionalism on Thorpe's part. . . . The reason why he himself did not give notice of his acts is explained by him on the ground of ignorance. In some justification of this position, it should be noted that Mr. Thorpe is an Indian of limited experience and educated in the ways of other than his own people. . . . The Amateur Athletic Union regrets that it permitted Mr. Thorpe to compete in amateur contests during the last several years, and will do everything in its power to secure the return of prizes and the readjustment of

points won by him, and will immediately eliminate his records from the books.

Carlisle Superintendent Friedman, regardless of the fact that he and Warner had released Thorpe to play ball four years before, wrote the AAU, saying:

> I hasten to assure your committee that the Faculty of the school and the athletic director, Mr. Glenn Warner, were without any knowledge of this fact until to-day. As this invalidates Thorpe's amateur standing at the time of the games in Stockholm, the trophies which are held here are subject to your disposition. Please inform me of your desires in the matter. It is a most unpleasant affair, and has brought gloom on the entire institution.

They had all neatly covered themselves and left Thorpe in the lurch. The American public lifted an angry voice. Why was Thorpe being singled out when so many other college athletes had also played semipro ball? They had been far more deceptive, after all, by using false names. In reply, the AAU assured the public that it would investigate college professionalism. The Union decided to return Thorpe's medals to the International Olympic Committee in Lausanne, Switzerland. But the IOC wasn't even sure whether it should take the medals back. The Olympic rules stated that objections to a participating athlete's amateur standing must be made within a month of the games. In Thorpe's case, the games were already a half year in the past.

In the southern states, the reaction to the discovery of Thorpe's secret was the same as Jim's. What secret? People there pointed out the newspaper stories about Thorpe that had been printed in local papers during the Olympics. The stories proudly, and prominently, mentioned the fact that he had once been a local baseball player, and a good one at that. Athletic officials across the country began to wonder why nobody had come forward to mention Thorpe's ball playing in all the years he was a national football hero or an Olympic sensation. Almost everyone was in agreement, including the *London Times*, which wrote, "Surely the standing of a competitor ought to have been discovered before and not after the Olympic games."

There was much sympathy for Thorpe from sports fans, athletic clubs and unions, and even international athletic committees all over the world, but the AAU was in no position to back down. The whole affair had already been embarrassing enough. The newspapers both in America and abroad lambasted the AAU for disgracing Thorpe and demanded a definition of "amateur," if indeed Thorpe wasn't one. The *London Daily News* said:

Is the Secretary of the American Amateur

Athletic Union satisfied that Thorpe ran straight and won straight when he carried off the Decathlon and Pentathlon prizes? If so Britain thinks none the worse of his baseball crime. Moreover, Britain is satisfied that Thorpe's victory was above board, even if Sullivan does not.

But it seemed obvious that nothing was going to change. Thorpe's medals were shipped back to Sweden; puzzled officials there held on to the medals until the International Olympic Congress convened in a May meeting. At Lausanne, Switzerland, the Congress decided that the AAU knew best how to handle its own athlete and that the medals should go to the runners-up in the pentathlon and decathlon. They were given to Ferdinand Bie and Hugo Wieslander by King Gustav at a ceremony in Sweden in June of 1913. There was "immense enthusiasm as three Swedish flags went up, and the Swedish total in the Olympic record was raised three points," reported the *New York Times*.

Thorpe was crushed. Yet the minute he gave up his awards in January, he knew that it was time to get on with his life—even if he never did know for sure what amateurism meant or just what he had done wrong. With Coach Warner acting as his adviser, he began bargaining with a number of professional baseball teams for a position. He might have been interested in a career in football, but professional football was practically nonexistent at that time.

Baseball, however, had already taken its place as the national pastime and was hugely popular. Thorpe was wooed by at least a half dozen ball club managers, but one made a more spectacular offer than the others. John J. McGraw, manager of the New York Giants baseball club, offered Thorpe some $5,000 for a one-year contract, then an outrageous sum for a rookie. Thorpe gladly accepted, and the agreement was announced in New York on February 1, when Thorpe signed his contract in the Giants' office.

Thorpe, the professional, gave a farewell to track sports that was to be long remembered. He appeared in a Boston meet on February 16 and, according to the newspapers,

> . . . in the open professional events won everything with the exception of the 40-yard dash . . . with ridiculous ease and in some he simply gave exhibitions, as the rest of the field, realizing the prowess of the Indian, did not care to compete with him.

The same day that Thorpe signed his Giants contract, he was discharged from Carlisle Indian School for the last time. It had been nine years since he had first enrolled, and his friends and teachers there must have seemed to him like family. In a way, that relationship was to continue. Iva

Miller, his school girl friend, and he were married in a Roman Catholic ceremony in Carlisle in October of 1913. It was a memorable event for the people of the town and for Carlisle's students, who knew him best. Superintendent Friedman gave the bride away; Gus Welch, the football quarterback and Jim's closest friend, served as best man. The ushers included Thorpe's friends from the football team and his younger brother, Ed, now a student at Carlisle. The evening ended with a dance in the school gymnasium. As Jim and Iva waltzed for the last time across the old wood floor to the strains of the school band, everyone's wishes for happiness went with them. They left the next day on their honeymoon on a goodwill tour of the world with the New York Giants.

Chapter 8

ENCORE FOR A CHAMP

Maybe Jim Thorpe would have signed up with a different ball club if he had known the Giants' manager, John McGraw, better. It wasn't that McGraw was a bad manager. After all, the Giants were the world champion baseball team, and McGraw was a successful, though strict, leader. His blunt, domineering personality worked to improve most players, but not Thorpe, who had an easygoing but self-reliant attitude. There was an unavoidable conflict between the two from the very start. Thorpe wanted to be his own man and learn the fine points of pro ball at his speed; McGraw wanted Thorpe to fit into a tight mold of rookie discipline and avoid standing out in the crowd. The manager didn't want any Olympic superstars distracting the rest of the team from their training and playing.

Ironically, one of the reasons the Giants' management wanted Thorpe in the first place was for his knack of standing out in a crowd. They knew that the world's greatest athlete would sell a lot of ball park tickets. But McGraw's own opinion was that Thorpe should be treated like the rest of the team and work his way up to "star" status one step at a time. That meant, among other things, a lot of time spent sitting on the bench. Unfortunately for Jim, the rest of the Giants were highly skilled ball players, and there just weren't very many instances where McGraw wanted to use a less experienced player like Thorpe.

When he did get to play, however, Thorpe was remarkably adept at the game, considering he had only played baseball for a couple of years in a very small rural league. He was a fine outfielder, with a good throwing arm. Up against the National League's finest pitchers, Thorpe was a competent batter and usually hit better than .300. Furthermore, his swiftness in track made him a fast base runner. It wasn't unusual for him to make first base even on an unspectacular hit to the field.

Jim and Iva started out life together by setting up the typical home of a baseball family. They had an apartment in New York City near the Polo Grounds, where the Giants played. Each spring, they traveled to training camp with the rest of the team, usually to Marlin, Texas, and socialized with the other baseball players and their wives. It wasn't long before they added to their small household. A boy, James, Jr., was born in 1915, two years after Jim signed with the Giants. Thorpe was enormously proud of his look-alike son and prized the time he spent playing with him more than any medals he could possibly have won. A happy family life took the edge off coping with manager McGraw each day.

McGraw was becoming increasingly displeased with

Thorpe's independent behavior. He was irritated, too, at Thorpe's favorite pastime—wrestling with the other players during friendly, off-hour matches at picnics and other gatherings. McGraw feared that one of his high-priced players would be injured in such horseplay and told Thorpe to either quit it or have his paycheck docked. As a result of their differences, Jim was beginning to spend more and more boring time on the bench.

Thorpe didn't allow himself to stagnate as an athlete, though. His love of football, his favorite sport, wouldn't let him stay away from the gridiron for long. Since the baseball profession left his fall and winter seasons free, he took a variety of part-time or seasonal coaching jobs at colleges. During the fall of 1915, for example, he coached football kicking at Indiana University. While he was working there, a friend from Carlisle—who was then playing with the Canton professional football team—paid Thorpe a visit. The friend came to offer Thorpe a position on the team called the Canton Bulldogs.

Professional football was in its infancy at the time but was becoming a popular game among the blue-collar working-class populations of the Midwest's booming industrial towns. Cities in Ohio were captivated by football—Canton, Toledo, Columbus, and Youngstown among them. So were towns in surrounding states. The game was being played by college and former college football players, with the ball club managers paying them for each game appearance. A number of top university players would come out to play under other names, either for the fun of it or to pick up some spending money. Former star athletes from the big eastern schools, along with one-time Carlisle stars, also were recruited to play. That is why manager Jack Cusack thought of Thorpe; if the big, former Carlisle Indian were to play, it would bring people from miles around to see the Bulldogs' football games.

Cusack offered a very sweet deal—$250 per game, which was a large sum of cash in those days—not knowing that Thorpe probably would have been delighted to play for much less money. Thorpe accepted the offer and played his first game with the Bulldogs in November of 1915. Cusack added Thorpe to the team just in time to surprise both the public and the Bulldogs' hottest rival, Massillon, Ohio, before the teams' big showdown. He was certainly right about Thorpe's drawing power. Whereas the average audience turnout had previously been 1,200, after Thorpe was signed attendance soared as high as 8,000. Thorpe was welcomed onto the field for each game with a loud cheer, and he must have felt good to be back as a football star at the age of twenty-eight, still in his prime.

During the first of two "world championship" games with Massillon, Thorpe thrilled the crowd with a few runs, including a forty-yard dash with the ball that brought Canton close to scoring. The Bulldogs, however, still ended up losing the first game. Then Cusack beefed up his collection of top players and named Thorpe team captain.

In their second game, Thorpe was the player of the day; two neat kicks sent the ball over the goalpost for field goals and put the Bulldogs ahead, 6-0. Massillon struck back in the last minutes of the game with a touchdown pass, but the receiver, who had to plow through a mob of spectators in the end zone, somehow lost hold of the ball. It was ruled a fumble, a decision so controversial that a ruckus between both groups of fans forced the game to be called, with Canton the winner. (Years later, Cusack found out that an overanxious Canton fan, who had bet thirty dollars on his favorite team, booted the ball from the Massillon receiver's hands, unseen by the officials.)

Thorpe was having a fine time. He was playing football again and was also seeing some of his old friends from his days in college ball. As more and more of his ex-Carlisle teammates were added to the team, playing with Canton was like attending an endless class reunion. Thorpe and his buddies went hunting on weekends in the wooded Ohio countryside, taking along Jim's favorite companions, two big Airedale dogs. During his spare time, Jim continued coaching for local colleges and even taught kicking to Pop Warner's college team at the University of Pittsburgh.

All this companionship added to Thorpe's zest for both the

game and life. Wrote Cusack, "On the field, he was a lovable fellow, big-hearted and with a good sense of humor."

Judging by one teammate's account of a typical hotel breakfast while on the road, Thorpe's zest for eating was also heightened:

> Jim would blow into the dining room about 10 and immediately be surrounded by waiters. He would always begin by saying he wasn't very hungry. This is what usually followed: grapefruit, cereal, half a dozen eggs with ham, sirloin steak with onions, fried potatoes, sausages, rolls, a pot of coffee.

Jim also enjoyed an occasional drink, like most of his athlete friends, and sometimes got a bit carried away. According to Cusack, that wasn't too hard to do; just a few drinks would put him out. But he never drank before a game and always drank in the company of his friends and teammates, who looked out for one another.

After his usual season playing baseball, Thorpe returned to the Canton team in the fall of 1916. The rivalry between Canton and the Massillon Tigers was more vicious than ever, and Thorpe spearheaded a team chock-full of former All-American football players. This superteam steamrolled its opposition early in the season, and fans throughout the Midwest eagerly awaited the two climactic Massillon games.

Some of the Bulldogs' victories were almost laughably lop-sided, with scores such as 67-0 and 77-0. Thorpe's involvement, according to Cusack, was not unlike that in the 1916 Cleveland game: "It was another great day for Thorpe, who carried the ball more than half of the time, did most of the kicking and passing, and thrilled the crowd of 7,000 fans with a 71-yard dash down the field after catching a punt."

The first of the two championship games with Massillon was frustrating for both fans and players. Playing on a slippery, muddy field, neither team could seem to get near the end zones, and the result was a scoreless tie. Both teams were raring to go at Canton the following Sunday, and a new player had been added to the ranks. It was Pete Calac, a Carlisle Indian who was a formidable fullback and a close friend of Thorpe's. The two dominated the game and, according to Cusack, "ripped the Tiger defense to shreds with their powerful drives." Both Thorpe and Calac scored touchdowns, helping Canton trample Massillon 24-0. Both players had proved that they were worth their huge salaries, for Canton was now the world champion.

The 1917 season was overshadowed by the nation's involvement in World War I. During the baseball season, Thorpe played with the Cincinnati Reds as an outfielder and saw a great deal of play. When he returned to Canton in the fall to play football for Cusack, he found that many of the sport's male fans and players had gone off to fight the war. The season went on anyway, and the Bulldogs again dominated the professional football scene with a vastly superior team. Since he was now doing almost all of the running and kicking in the game, Thorpe needed some help. He persuaded Gus Welch, his close Carlisle friend and best man, to come and play for $100 a game. In the annual games with the Massillon Tigers, the teams split. During the first game, Thorpe and Welch caught Massillon by surprise with their talent. According to Cusack:

> A striking example of the Bulldog power was given the 6,000 fans right at the start. Opening up on their own 23-yard line, Big Jim Thorpe and his eager helpers marched the ball down the field for seventy-seven yards without hesitating. It took just four minutes to travel the distance and send Thorpe across for a touchdown.

The second game was a surprise for Canton. The Bulldogs lost, 6-0, due in large part to Massillon's latest addition, Stanley Cofall. The big halfback was the closest Thorpe had come to meeting his match in recent years, and the game became a bitter duel between the two. The teams were closely matched, but Cofall managed to boot two field goals over the bar, shutting out the Bulldogs.

After the close of the season, Thorpe decided to return to Oklahoma with his wife and son, James, Jr. The Thorpes moved into a small home in Yale, Oklahoma, where they were to spend the next few years. In the fall of 1917 a daughter, Gail, was born. During the spring and summer, Jim was on the road playing baseball, and he spent his fall seasons in Ohio playing football. The result was that Thorpe spent less and less time at home.

In 1918, not long after the move to Yale, Jim, Jr., was stricken with a severe illness and died. The boy was only two and a half years old. Jim had experienced the death of close relatives before, but the loss of his son, the source of his pride and pleasure, simply devastated him. Friends and relatives, including his wife, Iva, later said that Thorpe was permanently changed by the event. He outwardly remained the same easygoing, friendly person, but an air of moodiness and personal loss, perhaps compounded by his humiliation as an ex-Olympian, sometimes hung about him. Thorpe's absences from home and the stories of his drinking increased.

Not long after that tragedy, Thorpe had his last run-in with Giants manager McGraw. During a game, Thorpe made an error that infuriated McGraw. The feisty manager called Thorpe an insulting name, a poke at Jim's racial pride that made something snap inside. Thorpe ran after McGraw and had to be held back by his teammates. McGraw dismissed him immediately, farming him out to the club's less famous triple-A teams.

Over the next several years Thorpe was moved from club

to club, and while he made a steady living at the game of baseball, he never quite fulfilled the potential he had had when he first signed on in 1913. Thorpe played in cities such as Portland, Maine, and Toledo and Akron, Ohio. He became a respected outfielder and always batted well, hitting consistently over .300 and sometimes as high as .358—enough to please managers and audiences.

Jim returned to Canton as both a player and coach for the Bulldogs in the fall of 1919. The thirty-two-year-old athlete was beginning to slow down a bit and was glad to bring in Joe Guyon, former Carlisle star, to play right half and help share the ball-running chores, along with Calac. They were an impressive sight on the field, and the team was good enough to beat most of its competition. Canton even triumphed in both Massillon games, a first for the Bulldogs.

The next year, 1920, Thorpe was named president of a new football group that intended to organize professional football and give strength to the fledgling sport—the American Professional Football Association. The title went to Thorpe in honor of all he had done to attract public attention to football. Eleven teams signed up: the Canton Bulldogs, the Rock Island Independents, the Rochester Jeffersons, the Buffalo All-Americans, the Decatur Staleys, the Chicago Cardinals, the Chicago Tigers, the Cleveland Panthers, the Dayton Triangles, the Hammond Pros, and the Akron Pros. All the towns were located in Illinois, Indiana, Ohio, and

New York; later the association would take on a wider scope under a different name—the National Football League.

Massillon did not buy a franchise in the new league—a disappointment to a lot of Ohio football fans. Without the cherished Massillon rivalry to follow, fewer of them turned out to watch the Bulldogs play that year. Thorpe and his team were having an off year, which did little to encourage fans to buy tickets.

Thorpe decided to call it quits with the Bulldogs after the season ended and went to play with the Cleveland Indians and the Toledo Maroons during 1921 and part of 1922. Later in 1922, he organized an all-Indian baseball team in Marion, Ohio, called the Oorang Indians. The team was sponsored by the owner of the Oorang Dog Kennels, from whom Thorpe obtained some of his Airedale hunting dogs.

The Oorang team provided another opportunity for Thorpe to assemble his old friends from Carlisle Indian School. Although the team didn't win many games, it had a lot of fun playing, and the enjoyment spread to the spectators. The fans realized they were witnessing some of football history's great names playing together, and that was a treat. The team often appeared in Indian costumes and sometimes performed Native American dances before games to help bolster attendance. Enough fans turned out to watch the Indians play to support the team for two seasons before it disbanded.

Thorpe spent the next few years filling in his off-baseball

months by playing football with a variety of teams, including the Canton Bulldogs. Age, and the many years of taking the physical punishment that went along with football, began to catch up with him. But he still had some great moments on the field and never failed to please crowds with his pregame punting exhibitions. Before the first quarter, Jim would place footballs in the center of the field and neatly kick one over each goalpost.

During play, he still could pose a threat to the opposition when the mood caught him. Ernie Nevers, the Stanford University All-American, recalled playing against the thirty-nine-year-old Thorpe in a Duluth-Canton game of 1926. Thorpe plowed into the young Nevers after a pass reception. As always, Jim helped the stunned player to his feet and asked him if he was okay. "Sure, Jim, I'm okay," Nevers said. "But I'm glad I wasn't playing against you ten years ago." He later related the truth: "I felt as though my ribs had been caved in, as if I'd been pile-driven three feet into the ground. Never before or since have I been hit as hard."

That year, 1926, was Thorpe's last season with the famous Canton Bulldogs. He played for a few more years, making his final appearance with the Chicago Cardinals in 1929, during a Thanksgiving game. Even Jim agreed that it was time, at the age of forty-two, to quit playing. But his name was still a household word, and Thorpe decided it made perfectly good sense to capitalize on that any way he could.

Chapter 9

TRADING ON THE PAST

In spite of his fame, the later years of Jim Thorpe's life were sometimes hard ones. Thorpe was leaving the professional sports arena just as the Great Depression struck, and it was not a good time for anyone, even the world's greatest athlete, to be looking for work. He now had three daughters, Gail, Charlotte, and Grace, adding to his responsibilities. The stress added to his marriage by his on-the-road life during the 1920s, along with the bitterness of James, Jr.'s, death, resulted in a divorce. Thorpe remarried two years later, in 1925. His new wife was Freeda Kirkpatrick of Ohio, who bore four sons, Carl Philip, William, Richard, and John, during the early years of their marriage. This pleased Jim greatly, for as much as he enjoyed his daughters, he was still very much wounded by his first son's death.

Wishing to begin his postathletic career with a clean slate, Thorpe sought reinstatement to the Amateur Athletic Union in May of 1929. But the AAU showed no interest in Thorpe's case. Daniel J. Ferris, national secretary of the organization, dryly observed, "After his long professional career in baseball and football, Thorpe hardly would have any grounds for seeking reinstatement as an amateur. . ."

Thorpe next turned to Hollywood, which at one time had made grandiose offers to him, as a possible source of recognition and income. He sold the rights to his life story very cheaply—for $1,500—to Metro-Goldwyn-Mayer, which never used them. He also agreed to appear in Columbia Pictures' *The White Eagle*, but backed out at the last minute. When the studio went ahead and used Thorpe's name in the film anyway, Jim attempted, unsuccessfully, to sue for $100,000.

Persisting in looking for an open door to the world of show business, Jim performed as master of ceremonies for a traveling footrace exhibition and even as the emcee for a dance marathon. In 1930, he managed to land a job at Universal Studios in a walk-on Indian role, and later he appeared in movies about football and baseball at MGM. But the work was unsteady, and Thorpe had to fill in with whatever jobs he could find in order to keep food on the table for his family. The *New York Times* caught him modestly digging dirt in Los Angeles for four dollars a day. The paper interviewed Thorpe briefly, impressed by the fact that the great athlete was still smiling:

> "I'm not through," he said today. Jim is a nonentity in a motley crew of diggers excavating for the new Los Angeles County Hospital. . . . After work Jim goes home to a very small cottage where Mrs. Thorpe, who also can smile,

and Philip, 4, and Billy, 2, wait for him. Sometimes at night Jim opens a big book and the little Thorpes are properly awed, as though understanding it all. The book contains many clippings and some photographs. . . . It's hard to find a reason for the present state of affairs of the smiling former athletic hero. "Guess it's an old story," he grins. "I liked to be a good fellow with the boys [lending his friends money]. But I'll come out of this, and I'll do some saving when I do."

Actually, he never did much saving. When he was a professional, Thorpe had never acquired much skill in handling money matters. Even though he was paid handsomely, he was nonchalant about lending money to friends and even acquaintances and never liked to ask for the money back.

During the 1930s, Thorpe drifted through a number of bit roles in Hollywood movies, some of them bigger than others. He decided to help other Indians interested in motion picture work and helped represent them in business dealings with the studios. Thorpe also discovered the avenue of public speaking, which opened to him when he was asked to give talks to children at various public schools. He always loved being around kids and enjoyed the attention, even if it did nothing for his wallet.

In 1937 Jim again raised his voice on behalf of his fellow Indians. His ancestral Sac and Fox tribe in Oklahoma had just voted to place control of Indian reservation land with the federal government and to have its people remain wards of the government, not typical American citizens. Thorpe complained:

> There hasn't been a single poor Indian helped by any of this legislation. The Indian who has the money is the Indian the government is always wanting to protect. We are trying to keep our tribe free from government meddling, to give the Indian a chance to stand on his own.

The effort to improve conditions for the Indians failed, but in representing his people, Thorpe found that he enjoyed public speaking. He accepted more and more speaking engagements. Represented by a booking agency, Thorpe began traveling across the country on a lecture tour. He traveled in an old car, taking with him an Indian costume that he used during his talks and his trusty hunting dog companions. Thorpe enjoyed talking about the sports scene, including glimpses of his athletic career, and about the ways of Indian life.

That kind of travel did not bode well for a married couple, and in 1941 Freeda sued for divorce. Thorpe continued with the lectures, which were becoming increasingly popular, and covered some seventy thousand miles in travel, right up to the onset of World War II. At that point, Jim wanted to do something for his country, though at fifty-four he was well beyond service age.

Thorpe was offered a job as a guard at the Ford Motor Company's River Rouge plant in Dearborn, Michigan, where military vehicles were produced. He and his four sons settled in the suburb of Romulus and Thorpe seemed to thrive on the steady work. But during his first year there, he suffered a heart attack. It was a warning to Jim that he was no longer a rough-and-ready youth and that he needed to slow down somewhat.

The incident put his name in the papers, which inspired the Oklahoma state legislature to seek a return of Thorpe's medals and restoration of his name in the record books. One member of the legislature even urged that Thorpe be appointed athletic director for one of Oklahoma's colleges, but the recuperating patient was in no position to move at that time. The state's plea to the AAU, like all other attempts made from time to time by fans and sportswriters, was flatly denied.

After recovering from his heart attack, Thorpe returned to Oklahoma. He wanted his boys to be raised in a stable environment and asked the Bureau of Indian Affairs to enroll them in the agency's Indian schools. The itinerant lecturer returned to his speaking engagements.

In the spring of 1945, Thorpe was married for the third time, this time to Patricia Askew, an admirer from Kentucky. The new Mrs. Thorpe was determined to help organize Jim's life and to make sure that he was properly compensated for his appearances. During the last years of his life, she saw to it that Jim's finances were in fair order and that he didn't end up a government charity case.

Still wanting to contribute somehow to the continuing war effort, Jim joined the merchant marine as a carpenter aboard an ammunition and supply ship. The papers reported that "Thorpe's wife disclosed that he joined last month following the enlistment in the navy of his son, Philip, 18." He sailed to the Indian Ocean that summer, and while the ship was supplying the front lines in India, Thorpe was asked by field command to speak before audiences of enlisted men. According to the army newspapers:

> Upon reaching downtown Calcutta, "Big Jim" was greeted by Brig. General Robert R. Neyland, Commanding General of Base Section. Tales of olden times when Thorpe, then with Carlisle, played against General Neyland, who performed with West Point, were once more renewed during their chat. Another gridder to meet Thorpe was a former member of the Chicago Bears' eleven, Capt. Chester Chesney,

Athletic Officer at Base Section Special Service Office.

Thorpe appeared before a number of GI audiences during his tour and was guest on an armed services radio sports program as well. At the end of the war, he returned to the United States and to more appearances for schools, clubs, association meetings, and banquets. He took a special interest in youth athletics programs, urging communities to initiate such programs as a first defense against juvenile delinquency. The city of Chicago hired him in 1948 to join its Park District staff. He taught kids the fundamentals of track and field and helped promote his idea for a Junior Olympics. While in Chicago, Jim took time to appear in an old-timer's baseball game at Wrigley Field and even batted a home run.

That year Thorpe was invited to San Francisco to be honored, along with Pop Warner and Ernie Nevers, in a sports tribute sponsored by a local newspaper. While there Thorpe even jogged onto the field prior to a San Francisco 49ers game to give one of his famous ball-kicking exhibitions. Wherever he went, people of all ages appreciated his relaxed, friendly manner of speaking and his trademark—a broad grin, so big that it made his sparkling eyes seem to close.

After having sat on the movie rights to Thorpe's life story

for so many years, MGM finally sold them to Warner Brothers in 1949. Warner began production of *Jim Thorpe—All-American* during that year and hired Thorpe as a consultant. Jim helped Burt Lancaster, who played the leading role, learn to handle and kick a football convincingly for the movie.

Fortunately for Warner Brothers, Jim's name was back in the public eye by the time the movie was released two years later. In January of 1950, the Associated Press poll of sportswriters and broadcasters named Thorpe the greatest football player of the first half of the century. Thorpe outdistanced the great Red Grange, Ernie Nevers, Bronko Nagurski, and others for the honor by a comfortable margin of votes. Jim was enormously flattered that he hadn't been forgotten, even as new and exciting football players stepped into the limelight each year. From the 391 people surveyed, Thorpe received 170 votes, as compared with 138 for Grange, 38 for Nagurski, and 7 or fewer votes for Nevers and dozens of other famous players.

But an even greater honor was bestowed the next month, with the Associated Press's selection of Jim Thorpe as "best male athlete of the half century." Thorpe outscored the competition by an even wider margin than before. This time broadcasters and writers were asked to name their first, second, and third choices for the honor; almost two thirds gave Thorpe their top rank. The closest runner-up, baseball legend Babe Ruth, tallied 539 points as compared with Thorpe's 875. Other contenders were fighter Jack Dempsey, with 246 points, and Ty Cobb, baseball hero, with 148. A total field of 56 athletes' names showed up in the poll.

News of the honors reached every part of the world, and hundreds of groups requested appearances by Thorpe. He was invited to a great many honorary banquets, was given the key to the city of Philadelphia, and was welcomed back to Carlisle and Canton for various celebrations. Thorpe was also entered in the National College Football Hall of Fame.

During the summer of 1951, he hit the road again with a traveling Indian entertainment program. While he was involved with this tour, Warner Brothers finally released *Jim Thorpe—All-American* with world premieres in Carlisle and Oklahoma City. Thorpe was on hand in Carlisle to see the film, along with the state governor and other celebrities. Carlisle's dignitaries had a monument to Thorpe's athletic achievements erected at the courthouse in time for his visit. The movie, though presenting a glossed-over account of Jim's life, did well at the box office.

The film drew attention to the fact that Thorpe had received little compensation for his life story. In fact, Jim and his wife were practically broke when he entered a Philadelphia hospital with lip cancer in November of 1951. Thorpe had discovered a lump on his lower lip, which was removed in surgery. Mrs. Thorpe admitted to the press:

We're broke. Jim has nothing but his name and his memories. He has spent money on his own people and has given it away. He has often been exploited. . . . In desperation, because of lack of funds, Jim and I assembled a bunch of Indians, dancers and singers. We hoped to launch a nationwide night club tour and opened the first engagement several weeks ago in Philadelphia. We have many bookings, but Jim won't be able to fill them in view of what has happened.

The prominent surgeon who performed the operation offered his services without charge. But he ordered Thorpe to stay in the hospital for ten days, with a period of recovery at home to follow. News of Thorpe's plight sparked action from a number of groups, including several Indians living in the New York area. Juanita Senter, a Sioux princess, formed a committee there to enlist aid. She donated one hundred dollars herself, in hopes that a fund would "help him get on his feet so that he can resume his work as soon as possible," she told the *New York Times*.

Warner Brothers, perhaps embarrassed by the situation, pledged money to the fund. Football players at Ohio State University in Columbus began a drive to collect their own fund, which soon reached $1,200 and more. Said the papers:

Among the donors were several Indians, one

named White Crow; two Alaskans who said they never saw Thorpe, but were thrilled by the stories of his feats; service men in all branches, some in the field and others in hospitals, ranging in rank from private to colonel; an Illinois Army private and his wife who were given a lift by Thorpe as they hitch-hiked to the Coast, and a host of plain, everyday fans.

Dallas broadcaster Bob Mayes, of station KLIF, described Thorpe's medical and financial condition to his listeners. Within hours he had solicited some five hundred dollars from several well-wishers. A month later, Thorpe was back on his feet.

During the Olympics of 1952 at Helsinki, Finland, Jim's name came up again, in a more flattering light. Paavo Nurmi, the Finnish track and field champion of three Olympic games, who had last competed in 1928, was an observer. "Jim Thorpe could still beat them all," he told reporters. "I think I could, too—but, of course, I can't be sure." Nurmi noted that the contemporary athletes were no better physically than Thorpe had been, but that they strived for perfection in single events instead of training for a variety of track events the way Thorpe and other early champions did.

Not long after the games, Thorpe suffered his second

heart attack in Henderson, Nevada, where he was admitted to the hospital in serious condition. Thorpe had been resting at home on August 8 when he complained that he was not feeling well and suddenly collapsed. He was placed in an oxygen tent at the hospital and kept under observation for several days.

Thorpe never fully recovered, and seven months later his once-strong heart finally gave out. He was eating dinner with his wife in their trailer in Lomita, California, when he fell unconscious. According to the *New York Times*:

> Mrs. Thorpe's screams attracted a neighbor, Cathy Bradshaw, who administered artificial respiration for nearly half an hour. A county fire rescue squad took over and was momentarily successful. Thorpe revived, recognized persons around him and spoke to them. He was conscious for only a brief time before he suffered a relapse and died.

Across the nation, newspapers carried the sad news on their front pages. Obituaries poured forth, praising Thorpe as an athlete and offering poignant reflections on Jim's inability in later years to achieve lasting happiness or security. And one more time, the insistence that Thorpe be reinstated as an Olympic champion was heard from all corners. The *Times* wrote in an editorial that in the final analysis, the stubborn, petty refusals of the United States Olympic Committee didn't really matter:

> What sticks, however, is the fact that in every form of athletics to which he turned, he was a magnificent performer. He had all the strength, speed and coordination of the finest players, plus an incredible stamina. . . . His memory should be kept for what it deserves—that of the greatest all-around athlete of our time.

Thorpe wasn't able to rest in peace for quite some time because of confusion and indecision on the part of Mrs. Thorpe as to where he should be buried. His body first was held in mortuaries in Lomita and Los Angeles in anticipation of his memorial service. Time was needed so that his daughters and his sons, who held various military posts, could be summoned. The body would lie in state, said a family friend, so that "everybody who wants to see him can—especially the kids. He helped so many become men."

During Thorpe's memorial service, a delegation of thirty Indians from Riverside County, California, was the first to view his body. By the end of the first day, several hundred had paid their respects to the fallen athlete, and the rosary was recited for Thorpe in the evening. The body remained in state for a few more days, and some three thousand people eventually visited.

Among them were teammates from the 1912 United States Olympic team; friends from the New York Giants and the Canton Bulldogs; and, of course, the Carlisle Indians, including Gus Welch, former quarterback and Thorpe's close friend. The Norwegian Sports Association was one of dozens of organizations that sent floral tributes.

Among the many condolences received from around the country was a telegram from President Dwight Eisenhower, who, as an Army cadet at West Point, had played against Thorpe. It read:

> I learned with sorrow of the death of my old friend, Jim Thorpe. I am delighted that as a tribute to his achievements and to his warm personality, a fitting memorial is to be erected in his memory. Jim has long been recognized as one of the outstanding athletes of our time and has occupied a unique place in the hearts of Americans everywhere. As one who played against him in football more than 40 years ago, I personally feel that no other athlete possessed his all 'round abilities in games and sports.

Two days later, the Oklahoma state senate voted to empower Governor Johnston Murray, part Indian himself, to select a five-person Thorpe memorial committee. Members would be in charge of selecting a memorial site, accepting donations, and supervising construction in Pottawatomie County, of which Shawnee was the seat. The city itself and the Sac and Fox tribe, headquartered near there, promised to build a $100,000 memorial near the high school football stadium. Furthermore, the school board voted to name the playing ground Jim Thorpe Memorial Field.

Patricia Thorpe agreed to have her husband buried there after receiving the promise of a large memorial and after the committee covered the expenses of transporting her, Thorpe's body, and his children to Shawnee. She had rejected an initial offer by the state to have the body placed in a shrine at the American Indian Hall of Fame in Anadarko, her reason being that she wanted a "separate, special memorial" for Jim. In the meantime, the governor of Pennsylvania and a Thorpe Memorial Organization were making plans of their own and clouded the issue by requesting permission from Mrs. Thorpe to bury her husband in Carlisle.

Thorpe's body arrived by train in Shawnee in a gilt casket on April 9 and was met at the station by several admirers who had known Thorpe locally when he was a boy. Secret burial rites, including a huge Indian-style feast, were held on April 13 by members of the Sac and Fox tribe. A high mass was then celebrated at St. Benedict's Catholic Church. The body was placed in a temporary crypt.

At some point, Mrs. Thorpe decided she would not wait for Shawnee to build its memorial for Thorpe. She was angered by the state legislature's failure to act on its agreement to provide funds for the memorial. When the rent on the crypt ran out, she had the body moved once again, this time to Tulsa. Patricia set out to find a fitting town in which Jim could be laid to rest, and her travels brought her to a tiny pair of Pennsylvania towns called Mauch Chunk (pronounced Mock Chunk, Indian for "Bear Mountain") and East Mauch Chunk. She convinced civic leaders to bring the two communities together under one name, Jim Thorpe, and to pledge the construction of a granite memorial for the body.

Townspeople thought it would be a good opportunity to settle the rivalry that had existed between the two communities and agreed to Mrs. Thorpe's proposal in May of 1954, more than a year after Thorpe had died. Thorpe's body was placed in another crypt until a red granite mausoleum could be completed some three years later. On Memorial Day of 1957, the monument was dedicated.

At each corner of the mausoleum a different packet of soil was scattered. One was taken from the land where the Thorpe family residence stood in Oklahoma; one was from Indian Field at Carlisle; another was from the Polo Grounds in New York, where Thorpe had played baseball. The fourth packet of earth was sent by the king of Sweden. It was soil from the track at the Olympic Stadium in Stockholm, where Thorpe had become an international legend.

Chapter 10

A FINAL MOVE FOR JUSTICE

Respect for Jim Thorpe and his achievements did not end with his death. Neither did the efforts to have the medals and trophies he won in the 1912 Olympics returned to American soil and his name cleared.

After Thorpe died, the National Football Association established its most valuable player trophy to be given each season to the most talented professional ball player. Fittingly, it was named the Jim Thorpe Award.

In 1958, Thorpe was elected to the National Indian Hall of Fame in Anadarko, Oklahoma, and three years later was included in the Pennsylvania Hall of Fame. He had already been written into the Oklahoma Hall of Fame in 1950.

When the National Professional Football Hall of Fame was established in Canton, Ohio, the sport's birthplace, in 1963, Thorpe was among the distinguished list of players named as charter members. Thorpe's name was later included in the National Track and Field Hall of Fame.

The battle to have Thorpe's accomplishments written back into the record books and to have his prizes returned was at last getting somewhere in the early 1970s. Thorpe was reinstated by the Amateur Athletic Union, the group that had acted to disqualify him in the first place, on October 12, 1973. Meanwhile the Thorpe family and their supporters had turned to the International Olympic Committee for a similar reinstatement, but president Avery Brundage held fast to his decision to refuse such proposals. Some people suggested he did so out of jealousy for Thorpe's talent; Brundage had competed alongside Thorpe, but not nearly as successfully, in 1912. But when asked about the matter, he would only say, "I do not have the power to change that judgment even if I wished." In reality, Brundage could have wielded considerable influence in Washington, D.C., to bring about a reversal. In 1972 Brundage retired.

In 1976 Jim's daughter Grace personally asked President Gerald Ford to have the Jim Thorpe issue discussed at the IOC executive committee meeting in Montreal, Canada, later that year. President Ford appealed to Lord Killanin, president of the IOC, "as a private citizen." The issue was brought up at the meeting and immediately tabled.

Thorpe's daughter Charlotte remained highly involved in the effort, and had been able to get the attention of the USOC and influence its decision to reinstate her father. But attempts to convince the IOC were fruitless. The IOC presidency eventually changed hands once more and was taken by Juan Antonio Samaranch of Spain. Ironically, it was two American delegates to the international committee who were most resistant to the idea of reinstating Thorpe. One of them showed little understanding of the situation and was even unaware that the AAU and the USOC had already agreed.

The Olympic bylaws concerning disqualification had been broken back in 1913. As the *New York Times* had pointed out in January of that year, "the rules of the Stockholm contests clearly prescribed that all protests against contestants on the ground of professionalism must be filed within thirty days after the distribution of the prizes." In fact, it was fully six months after Thorpe won his prizes that the AAU decided to seize them.

Paul Ohl, president of *Comité International Pour La Rehabilitation de James Francis Thorpe* in Montreal, wrote to the IOC in 1976 regarding the Stockholm rules.

Grace Thorpe asked Senator Alan Cranston of California to introduce a resolution to the United States Congress requesting that the IOC restore Thorpe's records and return the medals. This resolution passed in 1976.

Finally, William E. Simon, newly-elected president of the United States Olympic Committee, got involved. In October of 1982, Simon attended the executive conference of the International Olympic Committee in Lausanne, Switzerland— the city where Thorpe's prizes had been locked up some seventy years before—determined to clear up the Thorpe case. Simon cornered IOC president Samaranch beforehand

and bargained with him to bring up the Thorpe matter.

Samaranch did bring up the issue and made surprisingly short work of pushing through a decision to restore Thorpe's medals and amateur status, at long last. The many years of frustration had finally come to an end. Just as frustrating, in a sense, was Samaranch's answer as to why it had taken so long for the IOC to clear up the affair: "I don't know. For the first time since I became president we studied this problem, and we solved it in two hours."

Since the original medals had been given to the runner-up contestants in the pentathlon and decathlon, Ferdinand Bie and Hugo Wieslander, it was agreed that it would be unfair to take them back so many years later. So the committee decided to award duplicates of the medals to each of Thorpe's seven grown children.

Thorpe will have to share the record book with the two runners-up; the committee decided simply to add Jim's name as a cochampion, rather than rearrange the records to indicate his true accomplishments. The International Olympic Committee officially returned Thorpe's honors during a ceremony with his family in 1983. Gold medal replacements were given to Gail and Bill for all seven children, and silver replicas were given to all of the children— Gail, Charlotte, Grace, Bill, Dick, Jack, and Carl Philip, who was not present. In the audience were thirteen grandchildren and sixteen great-grandchildren of Jim Thorpe.

The family also expressed an interest in having their father's remains relocated to his Oklahoma homeland, "where they belong."

The Oklahoma Historical Society has restored Thorpe's home in Yale and it is open to the public. In 1984 the United States Postal Service issued a Jim Thorpe commemorative postage stamp. Thorpe's birthday is celebrated in Yale, Oklahoma yearly and part of the festivities include the Jim Thorpe Relays. Plans are underway for a great celebration on Thorpe's hundredth birthday, May 22, 1987, spearheaded by people in Yale.

The Thorpe family and Americans everywhere were encouraged by a sign that the same qualities that had brought Jim Thorpe success would endure. On May 8, 1984, they witnessed the ceremonial carrying of the Olympic flame on its way to the games in Los Angeles. The flame had been flown to New York from Greece. Two runners were given the honor of carrying the torch for the first kilometer (.62 miles) on American soil, as the flame's symbolic journey across the country began. One of the runners was Gina Hemphill, descendant of Olympic hero Jesse Owens. The other was Bill Thorpe, Jr., grandson of Jim Thorpe.

As Bill carried the flame high in front of him, his graceful legs moving as swiftly and purposefully as those of his ancestor, it seemed that the great athlete's heritage of excellence was as eternal as the flame itself.

Jim Thorpe 1887-1953

1887 Jim Thorpe (full name James Francis Thorpe) is born on May 22.

1889 The April 22 Oklahoma Territory land run deprives American Indians of vast acreage promised them by the United States government.

1890 President Dwight D. Eisenhower is born.

1893 Financial panic begins three years of economic depression in the United States. Over twenty-one million visitors attend the World's Columbian Exposition in Chicago. Jim Thorpe enters a federal Indian school at Stroud, Oklahoma.

1894 The International Olympic Committee is formed in Paris.

1895 The first officially recognized U.S. professional football game is played at Latrobe, Pennsylvania.

1896 The first modern Olympic games are held at Athens under the sponsorship of the king of Greece.

1897 William McKinley is inaugurated president of the United States as the country enters a period of territorial expansion. The death of Jim Thorpe's twin brother, Charlie, intensifies Jim's personal problems.

1904 Work begins on the Panama Canal. Jim Thorpe enters Carlisle Indian School in Pennsylvania, scene of his brilliant career in college football.

1908 Jim Thorpe wins acclaim in track-and-field events.

1912 At the Stockholm Olympics, Jim Thorpe wins the pentathlon and the decathlon and is hailed "greatest athlete in the world." On November 9 Jim Thorpe and his Carlisle football teammates defeat Army and West Point halfback Eisenhower. Jim Thorpe is chosen All-America halfback.

1913 Record-breaking track-and-field star Jesse Owens is born. Jim Thorpe is stripped of his Olympic prizes and standing and enters professional baseball.

1914 World War I begins.

1915 Jim Thorpe begins playing professional football at Canton, Ohio.

1917 The United States enters World War I.

1918 World War I ends.

1920 The American Professional Football Association (renamed the National Football League in 1922) is founded. Jim Thorpe is its first president.

1928 Herbert Hoover is elected president of the United States. Jim Thorpe plays his last professional baseball game.

1929 The American stock market crashes in October. Jim Thorpe plays his last professional football game, with the Chicago Cardinals on Thanksgiving Day.

1930 Two-time decathlon winner Bob Mathias is born.

1931 Economic depression becomes worldwide.

1937 Adolf Hitler outlines plans for German annexation of Austria and Czechoslovakia. Jim Thorpe begins a career as a public speaker on sports and American Indian topics.

1941 The United States enters World War II. Jim Thorpe spends war years as a guard in a military vehicle factory in Detroit.

1944 On June 6 the Allied forces under the supreme command of General Dwight Eisenhower invade Normandy.

1945 Jim Thorpe joins the merchant marine. The United States drops the first nuclear bombs on Japan. World War II ends.

1947 Middle-distance track star Jim Ryun is born.

1948 Harry S. Truman is elected president of the United States. Jim Thorpe begins work as a track-and-field coach for the Chicago Park District. Bob Mathias wins the decathlon.

1950 Jim Thorpe is named the greatest football player of the first half of the twentieth century. The Korean War begins.

1951 Julius and Ethel Rosenberg are convicted of transmitting United States atomic secrets to the Soviet Union and are sentenced to death. The film *Jim Thorpe—All-American* is released and becomes a commercial success.

1952 Bob Mathias wins the decathlon a second time.

1953 Dwight Eisenhower sworn in as president of the United States. Jim Thorpe dies on March 28 at Lomita, California.

1954 The National Football League establishes its most valuable player trophy, naming it in honor of Jim Thorpe.

1958 Jim Thorpe is elected to the National Indian Hall of Fame.

1963 Jim Thorpe is named a charter member at the founding of the National Professional Football Hall of Fame, Canton, Ohio.

1982 Jim Thorpe's Olympic medals and amateur status are restored.

INDEX- *Page numbers in boldface type indicate illustrations.*

125